The Curate's Lot

A. TINDAL HART

The Curate's Lot

The story of the unbeneficed English clergy

5 ROYAL OPERA ARCADE
PALL MALL LONDON SW1

© 1970 A. TINDAL HART

First published in 1970 by
JOHN BAKER (PUBLISHERS) LTD
5 Royal Opera Arcade
Pall Mall, London SW1

SBN 212 98380 6

Printed in Great Britain by
CLARKE, DOBLE & BRENDON LTD
Plymouth

Contents

Contents

Illustrations

PLATES

LIST OF ILLUSTRATIONS

LIST OF ILLUSTRATIONS

FIGURES IN TEXT

Preface

The story of the unbeneficed English parish clergyman should be of some interest both to historians and to the general churchgoer. For humble, despised, ill-treated and badly paid as he has been down the centuries, he, more than any other man, has bolstered up our famous parochial system and kept it going for more than a thousand years. Pluralist and non-resident incumbents called him in to run their parishes for them, bishops summoned him to fill the gaps caused by sequestration, sickness and deprivation, and to many a harassed and overworked rector or vicar he has proved a tower of strength, helping to bear the heat and burden of the day. Others have sat back and taken their ease, while he has done their work as well as his own. Yet he flits through ecclesiastical history like a wraith: unheeded, unsung, taken for granted, his faults and failings alone remembered. Usually a bird of passage, although there are plenty of exceptions to this rule, he has left few marks of his presence behind him, except in the hearts and souls of the men and women he served so faithfully. In the long run, of course, he would either blossom into an incumbent himself or be cast aside like a worn-out glove by the Church to which he had given the best years of his life. One of G. K. Chesterton's 'Secret People', who has never until recent times begun to take his rightful and honoured place in society, he could well, even in the not so distant past, have echoed the words: 'Smile at us, pay us, pass us, but do not quite forget, that we are the People of England, who have never spoken yet.'

Let us then listen to his voice and follow his odyssey; as like the ancient Roman actor he makes his bow: 'If I have ever pleased you, that is my reward; if I have ever offended you, I crave your forgiveness.'

11

CHAPTER I

The Medieval Background

In Anglo-Saxon England, prior to the Danish invasions, the spearhead of the Christian Church was not the parish as we know it today with its individual incumbent and his assistant curates, but the community life of the 'minster' or monastery. The dioceses were few and very large, being co-terminus with each Saxon kingdom, whose monarch would allocate land as required for Church purposes. The head minster would be the seat of the bishop, sited in the capital city, where he gathered round him his clerical household or familia; but many smaller ones were also dotted throughout the country-side, serving their own particular localities and ruled over either by an abbot or a provost. Such a minster would consist of a hedged or stockaded enclosure, surrounding land given to it by the king, and containing a small thatched church and a number of tiny dwellings inhabited either by monks or secular priests with other clerics in minor orders. There were also some nunneries with their staff of chaplains. In imitation of the organisation and mode of life of the cathedral familia, the priests in these minsters would celebrate mass regularly and all the inhabitants assist in singing the daily offices. There would be a school, whose primary object was to prepare young boys for the ministry; and missionaries were sent out into the surrounding villages to preach and say mass, to convert and baptise. Other members of the community would engage in estate management. The conversion of England was very largely the work of these minsters that grew rapidly in numbers up and down the country.

Gradually, however, the parochial system began to take root. The large minsters, especially in the Celtic north, started to found rural chapels on their outlying lands, which could be served from the mother house; and even to build village churches. Aelfled, abbot of Whitby in St. Cuthbert's time, for example, created a parish church at Ovington; while the great Midland monastery of Medehamstede, later Peterborough, established others at Breedon, Brixworth, Bermondsey and Woking. But the founding of most village churches was the work of thanes, who from the seventh century onwards began giving land, building churches, and appointing and maintaining the priests who served them;

Fig. 1. Foundation of a Minster.

an independent process that the Church as a whole quickly sought to bring under her own control. Such rural priests, it was demanded, must first be presented to the bishop for his approval and confirmation, who would then license them to their respective cures. Furthermore the Synod of Clofeshoh in 746 instructed the bishops, despite all the difficulties of travel and communication, to make annual visitations of all the parishes in their diocese; while the priests themselves were ordered to attend the diocesan synod, accompanied by their clerks.

The village parson had his own strips of land in the common field, usually double the size of those possessed by an ordinary labourer, for which he either paid rent or performed some service for his lord, and where he might well work himself or at any rate help with the haymaking and the harvest. His abode was a chamber over the porch of his church or else a small house of daub and wattle indistinguishable from others in the village. He received from his parishioners certain recognised offerings such as 'church scot', a penny from each hearth payable after harvest, and 'soul scot', due at each death. Tithes, the tenth part of everyone's income from whatever source, which had been sanctioned by Scripture, were at first only a voluntary gift; until in the tenth century under King Edmund's laws (940–46) they were made compulsory along with 'church scot' and 'plough alms', a penny from each plough in the parish. But King Edgar's Code, published nearly twenty years later in 962, insisted that the bulk of these payments should be made to the old minsters, the parish priests only being allocated a small proportion.

By the late Saxon period the village church had become a built-in part of rural society. The villagers paid their tithes, made their offerings, and confessed their sins to the priest; they attended mass on Sunday and brought their children to be baptised. In return, as the only educated man in this tiny community, the parson introduced into it what little culture, learning and civilised manners that he possessed. In this he was greatly helped by the church building itself which was often a fine structure either of wood or stone, its plastered walls covered with coloured scenes from Scripture or the lives of the saints, and containing such beautiful things as embroidered altar cloths and frontals, fine service books and silver vessels. Moreover he represented the forces of law and order, and personified the spirit of alms-giving and charity.

The duties of the clergy as defined by Saxon law were many and various: they were expected to preach the Word to their people and forbid them to follow heathen customs, to baptise all children within thirty days of birth, to supervise their parishioners' morals, to teach the Credo, the Lord's Prayer and the Ten Commandments, and to explain the meaning of the sacraments. They must hear confessions and impose penances, visit the sick, anoint them with oil and bring them holy communion when in extremity. Sundays and holy days were to be strictly observed, the seven hours of prayer constantly recited, the rogation and litany processions regularly undertaken, and above all the parson must be chaste and keep himself unspotted from the world. 'Avoid drunkenness,' he was told, 'and warn your people against it . . . eschew unbecoming occupations, as ale-scop or glee-man, but

Fig. 2. Consecration of a
Saxon Church.

behave discreetly and worthily; abstain from oaths and forbid them; not to consort too much with women . . . not to bear false witness or to be the confidant of thieves . . . not to have to do with ordeals and oaths . . . not to be a hunter or a hawker or a dicer, but to occupy yourself with your books as becomes your order.'

After the Norman conquest the parochial clergy at first were left largely undisturbed; but changes soon manifested themselves. For now the English Church was fully opened up to the Continent, where the Papal writ ran unchallenged; and the civil and ecclesiastical courts became separated, which gave to the clergy a privileged position that they successfully maintained against the monarchy until their final submission to Henry VIII in the sixteenth century.

It was an era of construction and reform. Cathedrals and parish churches were rebuilt in stone, and fresh ones came into being. Under their Norman owners the manors were enlarged and improved: much waste land was brought into cultivation and forest land cleared, which caused new hamlets to appear, which however remained subject to their original parish churches. These estates were frequently divided up between different members of a family, when the benefice might also be split into portions to each of which an incumbent could be instituted. Archbishop Langton in 1222 tried to put a stop to this practice, but vested interests proved too strong. The usual procedure was for the portionists, of whom there might be two, three or even four, to appoint a chaplain to do the work of the parish, to whose stipend they all contributed their quota, whilst retaining the bulk of the income for themselves.

The monastic system, which had fallen into decay in late Saxon times, now took on a fresh lease of life under the impetus of the Cluniac and Cistercian movements. Many new houses were founded by the Norman nobility; and this led to a profound and permanent change in the parochial system, i.e. the establishment of vicarages. For these patrons, along with lands and money, also endowed their monasteries with the parish churches in their gift, under the impression no doubt that monks would make good 'rectors' and adequately provide for the cure of souls, together with its attendant charities and hospitalities. But in practice this proved otherwise since monks were, generally speaking, ill-adapted to pastoral work, and instead of taking over these parishes themselves appointed chaplains on starvation wages to perform the minimum legal duties required, whilst annexing the greater part of the income for their own monastic uses. However at the Lateran Council of 1179 it was laid down that no monastery could receive tithes from the laity without the bishop's approval, who was also made responsible for the spiritual provision of such appropriated rectories. The Lateran Council of 1215 went further still. It pointed out that the average chaplain serving one of these parishes received no more than one sixteenth of the revenue, 'where it comes about that in these regions scarce any parish priest can be found who is even moderately well-educated'. So for the future, it decreed, the vicar, i.e. the rector's deputy, must receive a minimum wage of five marks and be given security of tenure. As a result the 'perpetual vicarage' came into being, where the *vicarius*, or rector's representative, was given a permanent and independent status. He was expected to reside, serve no more than one parish and be responsible only to the bishop. In return he must be adequately housed and paid. Normally he would receive all the tithes, except that on corn which would go to the appropriator (the owner of the benefice, frequently a monastery), together with the usual fees, offerings and a house. But not invariably so. Sometimes the vicar took the whole of the tithes and paid a fixed sum to the appropriators; sometimes *they* took all the income and gave him a fixed stipend; and sometimes he actually lived and ate at the monastery. None the less complaints continued to be made that vicars were underpaid and vicarages kept vacant for long periods in order that the appropriators might enjoy the full income; which led Archbishop Chichele in 1439 to demand that vicars should receive at least twelve marks a year.

A canon of 1268 had already decreed that vicarages must be filled within six months of a vacancy or else the presentation lapsed to the bishop. Under laws passed by Henry IV vicars were expected to be secular clergy, although this was not invariably enforced; but could be appointed whilst still deacons provided they proceed to the priesthood within the year. By the end of the thirteenth century half the English benefices had been appropriated, although all the appropriators were by no means monastic. Cathedrals, collegiate churches, bishops and even rectors all owned their appropriations. The last, for example, might appropriate his own rectory, converting it into a vicarage and securing most of the revenue for himself, whilst paying a vicar to do the duty. The Synod of Oxford in 1223 legislated against this practice, forbidding parsons thus to dispose of their parishes to others and demanding that before institution 'every presentee should make oath that he had not given or promised anything or entered into any agreement on account of his presentation'.

As new lands were brought into cultivation, new hamlets arose and new chapels were built, a struggle often developed to create new benefices independent of their mother churches. The first step was to secure the appointment of a resident chaplain, find him an adequate endowment and persuade the bishop to allow him to perform all the regular church services, plus the occasional services of baptism, marriage and burial. This was usually strongly resisted by the incumbent of the original parish, who sought to safeguard his rights regarding these new chapels. He expected the curate of such a chapel to take on appointment a vow of reverence and obedience to himself and guarantee a regular payment from his chapelry *in nominee subjectionis*. Furthermore he jealously reserved the right to perform all marriages and burials at the parish church; and demanded that the chapel congregation should attend that church on all the great festivals. Sometimes, however, if such hamlets happened to possess powerful patrons, who would press their claims, they might in the course of time become totally independent; but not many were so fortunate.

Absenteeism among the parochial clergy was widespread. Much of it was due to plurality, i.e. the possession of more than one living; but many rectors simply lived and worked elsewhere than in their parishes, whilst continuing to draw their stipends. A large number of such absentees were engaged in administrative or judicial work for the Crown, the nobility or the episcopate, and had been rewarded with more than one benefice, from which they drew the income but remained non-resident. Others included foreign rectors, who had been appointed by the pope, but dispensed from residence upon their benefices, which they regarded simply as a source of revenue; minors, who had also been granted a dispensation to continue their education at the university; domestic chaplains, whether of the nobility, gentry or the episcopate; clergymen, who were permitted to leave their parishes to go on a crusade, make a pilgrimage or visit distant estates; those, who were chronically sick or disabled through old age; and finally incumbents, who had no excuse at all, but preferred to live in idleness on the profits of rich livings, whose work could be performed by a stipendary chaplain on a starvation wage. 'If,' wrote Dr. Moorman in *Church Life in the Thirteenth Century*, 'a living were worth fifty marks a year, and a stipendiary chaplain could be found to do the work for an annual salary of three or four marks, the rector could enjoy a considerable income without the inconvenience of having to do any work. And many took advantage of this arrangement. As the bishops travelled round their dioceses they were constantly finding parishes totally neglected by their incumbents and left in the hands of ill-educated and sometimes quite inadequate stipendiaries.'

The education of the clergy as a whole was far from satisfactory and the vast majority were only partially learned; some indeed were practically illiterate, reciting the offices by heart but knowing little of their meaning. Their knowledge of the Scriptures was often ludicrously small, as when for instance one cleric mistook Barnabas for Barrabas and St. Jude for Judas Iscariot. Numbers of the Norman clergy, unlike their Saxon predecessors, who were men of good family and sound education, were drawn from the peasant class, whose only schooling might well be derived from some parish priest who himself was semi-literate. Relatively few of them found their way to the university and even when they did so their degree would be taken in general knowledge and not in theology, which was a post-graduate course reserved for a tiny minority of students. On the other hand certain bishops made a practice of sending men after ordination back to the university for special courses in theology, the Bible and canon law.

Schooling of any kind was hard to come by in country areas, but most towns could provide educational facilities; while the cathedrals, collegiate churches and the bigger monasteries often possessed institutions especially designed to qualify men for ordination or to prepare them for the university. The ordinary parish priest was expected, if possible, to keep a school and teach any promising boy what he himself knew free of any charge beyond anything which his parents themselves were voluntarily prepared to give him. The Council of Westminster in 1200 declared 'that priests shall keep schools in the towns and teach little boys free of charge. Priests ought to hold schools in their houses, and if any devout person wishes to entrust his little ones to them for instruction they should receive them willingly and teach them kindly. They ought not to expect anything from the relatives of the boys except what they are willing to give.' Sometimes professional schoolmasters were given benefices expressly for this purpose; and it was made illegal for any one to keep a school unless he were the parson himself, one of his assistants or the parish clerk. None the less it must have been difficult for a village lad to find the time to attend school and acquire any sort of education when the struggle for existence demanded that every able-bodied male from tender youth to gnarled old age should labour continuously in the common fields.

Such an educational system could hardly hope to produce highly-trained ordination candidates; but the bishops perforce had to put up with it in order to fill the yawning gaps at a time when probably a third of the male population was in holy orders. Necessarily they were drawn from all classes : the sons of small land-owners and yeomen farmers as well as the off-spring of craftsmen, tradesmen, and peasants. Chaucer's 'poure persoun' out of *The Canterbury Tales*, it may be remembered, had a brother who was a ploughman and a carter of dung. By the thirteenth century even the servile classes were not excluded, and it was possible for a man born and bred as a slave to rise high in a Church that prided itself on its classlessness, provided always he could obtain his lord's permission and a dispensation from the bishop, *de defectu natalium*, to go ahead to ordination. A serf, indeed, was expected to pay his master a fine in order to obtain leave to send his son to school, but this was frequently remitted by a kind-hearted lord who took a personal interest in a promising boy to whom he would ultimately give his freedom. These ordination candidates were encouraged to work hard by writers like the author of *Symon's Lesson of Wisdom for Children*, who dangled before their eyes the glittering prizes of the clerical profession :

> Lerne as fast as you can,
> For our byshop is an old man,
> And therfor thou must lerne faste
> If thou wilt be a bishop when he is past

Certainly many bishops were of humble origin like the famous Robert Grossetete of Lincoln.

Minor orders were frequently conferred when the better-class candidate was studying at the university or his poorer brother was acting as parish clerk to the parson who had educated him. But the two 'sacred' orders of deacon and priest could not be conferred until the canonical age of twenty-three and twenty-four respectively; and they also required a title, i.e. the promise of a definite job in the ministry or the possession of a sufficient income to insure the candidate against possible destitution, since the beggar priest brought nothing but disgrace upon the Church.

The numbers ordained were very large in order to keep up a constant supply to parish and monastery, which also involved a constant flow of episcopal dispensations, not merely from servile condition but illegitimacy, physical blemish, insufficient learning, etc. For if the supply was to meet the demand the bishops could not be choosers. The parish church itself was a thing of beauty. By now it was being built of stone and constantly enlarged: Norman architecture giving place first to Early English and then to the Perpendicular styles. The plastered walls were covered with paintings from the Scriptures and the lives of the saints; the windows were filled with stained glass; the chancel screen and rood loft were alive with their sacred figures; and the altar glowed with its rich coloured frontals and hangings, lit up by its many lighted candles. The parishioners were responsible for repairs to the fabric of nave and tower, and also apparently for all church furnishings. Archbishop Gray's register, circa 1250, declared:

We ordain and appoint that the parishioners provide a challice, missal, the principal vestment of the church, *viz.* a chasuble, white albe, amice, stole, maniple, zone, with three towels, a corporal, and other vestments for the deacon and subdeacon, according to the means of the parishioners of the church, together with a principall silk cope for the chief festivals, and with two others for the rulers of the choir in the aforesaid festivals, a processional cross and another smaller cross for the dead, a vase for holy water, an osculatory, a candle stick for the Paschal candle, a thurible, a lantern with a bell, a Lent veil, two candlesticks for the taper bearers; of books, a legendary, Antiphonary, Gradual, Psalter, Topiary, Ordinale, Missal, Manual; a frontal to the great altar, three surplices, a suitable pyx for the 'Corpus Christi', a banner for the Rogations, great bells with their ropes, a holy font with fastening, a chrismatory, images in the church, and the principal image in the church to whom the church is dedicated.

The Sunday mass at 9 a.m. was preceded by mattins and succeeded by an afternoon evensong. The two latter were badly attended, especially the last since the people who had gone home for midday dinner were either reluctant to travel the sometimes considerable distance back to church or else were lured away by the games, sports and merry-making which constituted such a considerable feature of the medieval Sunday afternoon. Mass itself usually saw a full church; but there was little reverence: the priest mumbling the service at the distant altar, while, divided from him by the length of the chancel, the laity stood about talking, laughing, even playing games, and taking no part in what was going forward at the altar except to kneel and turn their faces to the east in a sudden hush at the elevation of the host. They rarely communicated, probably not more than three or at most twelve times in the year, when everyone over sixteen years of age, whether confirmed or not, received the wafer. They did not expect to have to fast or to be given the chalice, although they might be allowed a draught from an unconsecrated cup to prevent any fragments of the wafer remaining in the mouth. After each celebration a 'holy loaf', blessed by the priest, was distributed to the congregation, which they took away to their homes. The children were catechised at evensong. Sunday work was strictly forbidden by Canon Law, but this prohibition was all too often honoured more in the breach than the observance. Piers Plowman's exhortation to cease all labours on a Sunday and attend one's parish church is, of course, well known:

> And upon Sundays to cease, God's service to hear,
> Both Matins and Masse, And after meat in churches
> To hear their Evensong, Everyman ought.
> Thus it belongeth to Lord, to learned and to lewd,
> Each Holy day to hear Wholly the service,
> Vigils and fasting days Further to know.

For holy days, the only holidays people then had and of which they made the most, also had their regular services; and from the thirteenth century onwards there was a daily mass at which there might be a small congregation of the pious. The clergy themselves were expected to say all the canonical hours; but this obligation was frequently neglected. Sermons were rare since they depended upon a knowledge of the Bible that few priests possessed, although they were expected to preach at least four times in the year. Instead the average incumbent would give a simple instruction on the Creed, the Lord's Prayer and the Ten Commandments, together perhaps with moral exhortations. The Procession of the Litany, which took place on certain Sunday afternoons, was generally popular, especially when it was preceded by a penitent in a white sheet, bearing a taper. It was, however, through the occasional services that the priest was brought most closely into contact with his parishioners. Infants were taken to the font immediately after birth and confirmed, if possible, a few years later. The marriage service, which was long and elaborate, concluded with the nuptial mass and a visit from the priest to sprinkle the happy couple in bed with holy water. The hearing of confessions entailed a great deal of work, since he was expected to conduct a long and searching examination into the lives of his flock in preparation for the Easter Mass. The visitation of the sick was yet another arduous task, when clothed in his surplice and preceded by his clerk carrying a cross and lantern and ringing a bell, he walked to their homes once a week. The burial service was a very solemn affair, an occasion when mass might be celebrated twice on the same day. The 'Bede Roll', a list of those who had recently died, was read out each Sunday, and they were commended to the congregation for their prayers. People sometimes left a small legacy to the church so that they could be commemorated each year on the anniversary of their death. Another of the parson's jobs was to pronounce a general sentence of excommunication twice or thrice in the year with bell, book and candle, against all robbers, usurers, slanderers, heretics and those who had broken the peace of the Church or refused to pay their tithes. For this purpose all the parishioners met together, 'then the candle is to be thrown down and the priest to spit on the ground and the bells to ring'. On the whole the average incumbent worked hard and carried out his duties faithfully; but also no doubt some neglected them, preferring to cultivate their glebes or take their ease at the ale-house.

Until the eleventh century when Pope Hildebrand enforced their celibacy the clergy had been allowed to marry. Then the fourth Lateran Council in 1074 not only forbade it, but pronounced excommunication against those who refused to put away their wives, and prohibited their sons from succeeding to their benefices. Naturally there was strong resistance and the majority of clergy continued to live, in a sort of morganatic marriage, with one woman, whose children were presented to the world as his nephews and nieces. Concubinage of this type, since it was too widespread to be stamped out, was largely ignored by the Church Authorities, the more so as the off-spring of such unions would be illegitimate and could not inherit or succeed to anything. None the less sons of the parsonage were often able to obtain an episcopable dispensation and so proceed to ordination, while daughters, despite their tainted birth, were eagerly sought for in marriage. Chaucer's Miller, for example, boasted of such a connection :

A wife he hadde commen of noble kin,
The parson of the town her father was.

The income of the average medieval rectory was around the £10 mark; but the out-goings were heavy. These included taxes to Rome in the form of first fruits and tenths, subsidies granted to the king, synodals and procurations due to the bishop and archdeacon, the wages of the clerical staff, the upkeep of the chancel, the obligation to provide hospitality and poor relief, the considerable expense involved in collecting their tithes and perhaps even a pension to a predecessor. This last had to have the sanction of the bishop and usually amounted to one third of the gross stipend of the living; alternatively an aged parson, when unable to carry out the duties, might employ a chaplain while continuing himself to reside at the parsonage. Sometimes, however, a pension was imposed on a benefice for another reason, to reward royal servants. The rector, who received all the tithe and farmed his own glebe, could usually make a comfortable living even in times of bad harvests and rising prices. The vicar, on the other hand, was usually not so fortunate, whether his income was derived from a fixed salary or the lesser tithes. Apart from the tithe an incumbent was entitled to various offerings and dues from his parishioners. These included congregational contributions at the greater festivals, the mass pennies of the faithful at the celebration of the Eucharist on Sundays, fees for the occasional offices, collections taken from penitents making their confession, the right of the priest to the loaves of bread and wax candles that remained over from the public services, mortuary dues payable after each death, the small legacy to which he was entitled in return for the drawing up and witnessing of a will, the plough penny from each plough team in the parish, and various other small but vexatious taxes, most of which were abolished at the Reformation.

One of the chief complaints against the clergy throughout the Middle Ages was that they behaved like laymen : farming their glebe to the neglect or the mere perfunctory performance of their duties; engaging in sports like hawking, hunting and fishing; and even gambling, dicing and drinking heavily in the village alehouse. Above all, dress was a bone of contention, with so many clergy refusing to wear the clerical habit or submit to the tonsure. An injunction of John Stratford, archbishop of Canterbury, in 1342 declared :

Parsons holding ecclesiastical dignities, rectories . . . benefices with cure of souls; even men in Holy Orders, scorn to wear the tonsure, which is the crown of the Kingdom of Heaven and of perfection, and distinguish themselves by hair spreading to the shoulders in an effeminate manner, and walk about clad in a military rather than a clerical dress, with an outer habit very short and tight-fitting, but excessively wide, with long sleeves which do not touch the elbow; their hair curled and perfumed, their hoods with lappets of wonderful length; with long beards, rings on their fingers, and girded belts with precious stones of wonderful size, their purses enamelled and gilt with various devices and knives hanging at them like swords,

27

their boots red and green, peaked and cut in many ways; with housings to their saddles, and horns hanging from their necks; their capes and cloaks so furred, so rash disregarded of the Canons, that there appears little or no distinction between clergymen and laymen.

But all attempts at getting the sumptuary Canons enforced proved futile. A fashionable head-covering, known as the 'priest's bonnet' was very popular since it was especially designed to conceal the tonsure; and this was worn with a coloured habit and a sword or knife hanging at the girdle in place of the string of beads. William Langland roundly condemned such practices :

> Sir John and Sir Geoffrey have a girdle of silver,
> A dagger or a knife with studs guilded.
> But a breviary that should be his plow.

Robert Grossetete, bishop of Lincoln, once refused to institute a deacon who came to him 'untonsured, dressed in scarlet, wearing rings, in the habit and carriage of a layman or knight, but almost illiterate'. Another bishop, having read out the relevant canons at a visitation, ordered that the hair of his clergy should be cut there and then.

Clergymen are but human and as subject to the lusts of the flesh and the vanities of the mind as anyone else. Certainly the medieval priest was no exception. Yet on the whole, despite their poverty and isolation, the vast majority of rectors and vicars were faithful to their ordination vows and worked hard in their parishes; not only carefully fulfilling their pastoral and liturgical duties, but by their personal piety and christian way of life, setting a shining example for their people to follow.

CHAPTER II

Assistant Clergy, Chantry Priests and Household Chaplains

The number of assistant clergy, chaplains or stipendiaries as they were then called, was very large; since out of about 40,000 ordained men in the secular ministry not more than about 900 were incumbents. This meant that each parish had its staff of curates, sometimes as many as seven or eight, and not usually less than two or three. Bishop Robert Grossetete in the thirteenth century expected to find in each parish at least a deacon and a subdeacon; and even the poorest benefice had its parish clerk. The Constitutions of Oxford, promulgated in 1222, demanded that the more populous livings should keep at least one extra priest and preferably more in case of illness or infirmity; but the bulk of the staff would consist of deacons and subdeacons helped out by boys or youths in minor orders—those of doorkeeper, lector, exorcist and acolyte—who would sing in the choir and assist in other simple ways for a little pocket money or on a purely voluntary basis, while they continued their studies under the incumbent or one of his chaplains. Few even of the chaplains in the major orders of priest, deacon and subdeacon were graduates, and many were no more than semi-literate, whom the bishops had ordained without enquiring too closely into their qualifications or whether they had more than a fictitious title, i.e. sponsored by some religious house that had no real intention of supporting them. These men at first had to exist as best they could on whatever casual employment came their way, as for example singing occasional masses for the dead, helping out in cases of sickness or infirmity, or taking the odd baptism and funeral, until they could find permanent work as annual chaplains under an incumbent. Then their principal functions would be regularly to sing the canonical hours, attending their rector in the chancel of the church clad in surplices provided at their own expense; and to assist him at mass, when under his direction they would read the epistle and gospel for the day. They were further expected to instruct the youth of the parish, to visit the sick and impotent, and to relieve the poor with parish alms. But perhaps the hardest working church official of all was the parish clerk, in minor and possibly in transit to major orders, who prepared the church for the services, helped with the singing of the offices and the administration of the sacraments, taught in the school and conducted the priest to the homes of the sick, carrying cross and lantern, and ringing a bell as he went. There is a typical account extant of his duties at St. Stephen's, Coleman Street, in London early in the sixteenth century, where he laid out the service books in the choir open at the necessary places, and collected them afterwards, served the vicar and other priests with their copes, kindled the censers, lit the candles and conducted the singing of the children in the choir. Twice a year he cleaned out the font and renewed the holy water, every Sunday he carried holy water to the sick and helped the sexton ring the bells, and it was his job to keep the clergy informed of any marriages, christenings or burials during the week and to attend the services.

Annual chaplains were very poorly paid as a rule; not more indeed than was sufficient to induce them to serve at all, since the less they received the more the incumbent could retain for himself. But there were of course exceptions that proved the rule. At Barnburgh near Doncaster, where two assistant priests, two deacons and two subdeacons were employed, the canons of Southwell paid the priests £8 each, the deacons £4 and the subdeacons £3 6s. 8d. per annum; while at the opposite end of the scale the dean of Salisbury during the year 1220 found that the chaplain of Arbonfield chapel in the parish of Sonning was only receiving 20s.

Attempts were made by the bishops to secure a recognised

minimum. Richard of Chichester decreed in 1246 that chaplains' annual stipends should be at least five marks, i.e. £3 6s. 8d; and Peter Quivil of Exeter some forty years later demanded £3 for priests in charge of parishes and 50s. for assistants. The principal reason behind these and similar injunctions was to prevent the degradation of clergy, who might otherwise, in lieu of an adequate stipend, be compelled either to beg, to engage in sordid secular pursuits or to dishonour their profession by going about indecently clad and so parade their poverty to the world. But it was found impossible always to enforce them. The unskilled labourer could earn as much as 40s. or even 48s. per annum; and all too many chaplains got little more. After the Black Death, however, it became a very different story, when owing to the greatly reduced number of clergy the laws of demand and supply began to operate in their favour. Now the ecclesiastical authorities sought to restrain rather than support their claims. Archbishop Islip tried to limit the stipend to six marks; but in 1378 Archbishop Sudbury, after deploring the greed of assistant priests, was compelled to allow them seven or eight marks. Still wages continued to rise and a statute of Henry V conceded a maximum of nine marks, provided that this amount was licensed by the bishop. The norm was in the region of eight marks, or four marks with food, for a chaplain with an independent cure of souls, i.e. in charge of a parish during the incumbent's absence or of an outlying chapel of ease; while the 'annualers', those assisting a resident incumbent at the parish church, received seven marks, or three marks with food. By the beginning of the sixteenth century the average stipend, probably less rather than more, was £5 3s. 2d. The curate of Calverton in Lincolnshire drew an income of £4 13s. 4d.; but another at Leckhampstead in the same diocese was paid £6.

How far were these salaries adequate? The domestic accounts of the two chantry chaplains at Bridport from 1453 to 1460 show that they were able to live very comfortably and entertain extensively on the incomes allowed them under Henry V's statute, besides paying the wages of a servant and keeping themselves in clothes. But most assistant parish clergy resided with the incumbent at the parsonage where they shared expenses in food, fuel and servants' wages, whilst finding their own clothes and paying for their own amusements such as they were. But if, as sometimes happened, an assistant curate had to find his own accommodation, in a layman's house or even in the village tavern, there would be an additional cost of 6s. 8d. per annum by the end of the fifteenth century. Perhaps too he had to support aged parents or other relatives; and in such cases the minimum of £5 would hardly have sufficed. For high taxation and the rapid rise in the cost of living had now to be taken into account. Charitable subsidies in aid of the archbishop were payable in the Canterbury Province from the mid-fifteenth century, which mulcted chaplains of 6s. 8d. per subsidy; while Cardinal Wolsey in the Northern Province instituted an annual levy of a fifteenth on the unbeneficed that worked out at 5s. 4d. on an income of £4. By 1520 prices had reached an average of 39 per cent above the mid-fifteenth century level and continued to rise at a time when wages remained relatively stable. Moreover many assistant clergy at this date were not even receiving the maximum rate laid down by statute. So in order to live chaplains were often compelled to supplement their income as best they could : by occasionally celebrating masses for the dead, attending funerals where they might receive a small dole, and engaging in such secular employments as trading or farming land on lease, for few curates possessed land of their own. No wonder they left little behind them when they died. The curate of Leckhampstead mentioned above, whose stipend of £6 was above the average, and who died in 1521 left property worth no more than £2 17s. 9d., the most valuable items of which were a gown (18s.) and three mares (£1).

The chaplain, unlike the rector and vicar, did not possess the freehold or indeed any kind of legal security of tenure; although it was generally understood that he could not be removed without reasonable cause, just as he must not be retained if he was found to be practising immorality. On appointment he took an oath of obedience to the incumbent or his deputy not to encourage or countenance any prejudice, scandal or gossip against him, and strenuously to uphold his rights and those of the parish church. The breaking of any part of this oath courted instant dismissal.

The vast majority of chaplains were of humble origin, whose relations were peasants, craftsmen and even serfs. Few could expect ever to be promoted to a benefice, and remained all their lives in an endemic state of economic insecurity and social subservience. Out of forty-two Leicestershire curates in 1517 only three ever secured benefices; and out of 112 men ordained priest in the same diocese of Lincoln only twenty-eight had received livings by 1526. Many served the same parish for long periods. Four curates who went to Boston in 1500 were still there twenty-six years later, and the same story is repeated in the neighbouring benefices of Grantham and Fulstow. The best off were those who were appointed to outlying chapels, where they sometimes had a small endowment and enjoyed comparative independence and security of tenure; or who were placed as deputies in charge of parishes from which the incumbent was absent for one reason or another, or because of chronic ill-health, old-age, etc., was incapable of carrying out his duties. It has been estimated that a quarter of all the parishes in England were held by non-resident incumbents, who had to provide such a deputy; while in many appropriated churches, where no vicarage had been ordained, the entire cure of souls as a 'perpetual curacy' was committed into the hands of a chaplain. Licences were often granted to the inhabitants of hamlets to build their own chapels, when they were usually allowed, with the approval of the incumbent of their parish church, to choose their own chaplains, whose stipends would be found out of their offerings. The mother church, however, jealously guarded her rights. The chaplain could take all the Sunday services and celebrate daily mass; he would baptise,

c

hear confessions and administer the last sacraments to the dying; but marriages and burials had to take place in the parish church, which likewise claimed all tithes, mortuaries and oblations. Each hamlet too had to contribute its quota to the repair of the church's fabric and the upkeep of its grave-yard; and its inhabitants must regularly visit the mother church on all the great feasts of the year, including those of its dedication and patronal festival. None the less such chaplains possessed a good deal of independence, as within certain carefully defined limits they might do more or less what they pleased, and could not easily be dismissed against the wishes of their congregations who supported them financially. Some of these chapels were endowed with gifts of land, and occasionally individual priests serving them were left legacies by grateful incumbents. For example Thomas Whitley, vicar of Marske in Cleveland, left money in his will of 22 January 1516–17 to 'Sir Richard Grymesby my priest'; and William Appilton, vicar of Huntington near York, made a similar bequest to 'Sir John Dalle my parish preste' on 17 December 1517.

Not unnaturally considering their origins, education, poverty and insecurity some of these chaplains proved unsatisfactory, although not as many as might have been expected when we remember that large numbers of them were left for long periods in independent charge of livings whose incumbents were absentees, where they were under no sort of supervision. In the large diocese of Lincoln between 1495 and 1521 only sixty parishes out of 1,700 complained of misdemeanours by their chaplains. The number of offences committed by incumbents was far higher.

'A curate,' writes Mrs. Margaret Bowker in *The Secular Clergy in the Diocese of Lincoln*, 'might well serve a cure better than the proper incumbent, whose powerful friends or influential relations might render him immune from the censures of ecclesiastical authorities.'

The accusations, where they were made, consisted of drinking heavily in taverns, neglecting their duties or performing them at the wrong times, not sleeping in the parish, failure to preach and visit, wearing the wrong clothes and having no tonsure, engaging in secular occupations, poaching, hunting, participating in rustic sports, fishing and gambling, and above all indulging in sexual offences. Sometimes they were held up to ridicule as fools or ignoramuses. It is possible that it was a parish chaplain who composed the bibulous medieval song which begins : ' 'Tis my intention, gentle sir, to perish in a tavern'. For deprived by their poverty of books and the opportunities for study, with few home comforts and no wife, they almost inevitably gravitated to the village ale-house during their brief leisure hours, where after a hard day's work in the fields or about their pastoral duties, they could unashamedly mix with men of their own class, enjoy its warmth and good fellowship, and drown their sorrows in a friendly atmosphere.

The curate of Newton Purcell in Oxfordshire admitted in 1530 to officiating only on feast days; and another at Spalding, Lincolnshire, in 1519 took no account of time :

Sometimes parishioners who came to mass and the hours found them finished, sometimes they had to wait. He would not go to the house of a deceased parishioner to accompany the funeral procession unless he was paid two pence. There were several charges of incontinence against him. His slackness affected the whole parish.

A third chaplain at Loughborough refused to visit the sick and give them the sacrament. He preferred to go fishing and fowling. Others immersed themselves in secular employment : John Adams of Quodring was accused of being a common farmer and merchant, and living incontinently; and a colleague at Surfleet did likewise, besides celebrating mass at the wrong times. Thomas Phillips, curate of Wootton near Woodstock, kept sheep in the churchyard, and a parishioner coming to make his confession found him shoeing a horse. Sir Richard, curate of Hawridge, was a muscular christian who diced and played football. He got through all his services including compline before 8 a.m., thus leaving the rest of the day free for recreation. Sir William, curate of Hardwick, Leicester, not only conducted his services irregularly, but was hot-tempered and quarrelsome to boot. He drew his sword at the slightest provocation and used his fists freely. Sir Agnus, a chaplain at Fulstow near Louth, was another common brawler, who was to be seen daily in the village tavern. Sir George, curate of Barton on Humber, was reputed to be 'a common fisherman and went out wading'; and at Fleckney the chaplain allowed his hair to grow long and wore clothes unsuited to his calling. And so the sorry tale continues with priests refusing to bury, to visit the sick, to give the last sacraments, to christen or to teach. In 1530 the curate of Henley-on-Thames became intimate with a married woman, Alice Christmas, and had the audacity to call her child 'his spiritual son'; whereupon he was abjured by the bishop's commissary 'to avoid her as he would the plague'. Another curate, Robert Becket, assaulted the wife of a certain William Tailboys declaring 'he must nedes have his pleasure of her', and when reprimanded by the churchwardens called them 'false perjured churles'. The parish was so incensed that two girls brought him a 'bale of clowtes' and asked him to christen it; but he escaped with no more than an exhortation from the diocesan chancellor to avoid feminine society in the future, while his parishioners were advised 'to live charitably together'. At Dawlish in 1301 it was reported of one of the chaplains: 'he hath kept his concubine for ten years or more; and although often corrected on that account, he incorrigibly persists'. About the same date another curate at Clyst Honiton, also in Devonshire, was said to be intimate with three different women at once, 'one of whom he keepeth and has long kept'. But perhaps the most colourful story was that of John Roo, curate of St. Christopher's next the Stocks in London, who stoutly denied the charge when one of his parishioners accused him of being the father of her child and sued him for £800 maintenance! And not content with this exorbitant demand took the opportunity of

a well-filled church one Sunday morning to march up the aisle
to the chancel in the middle of the service and lay the howling
babe down in front of him.

The illiteracy of many chaplains was a scandal and a byword.
There was a priest already mentioned who imagined that Epiph-
any was either a man or a woman; and in the winter of 1517–18
the curate of Whipsnade so mixed up the Church's seasons that
his parishioners were eating flesh in the Ember days before Christmas and the oblations of Candlemas were deferred until after the
beginning of Lent. At the dean of Salisbury's visitation of Sonning in 1220 it was discovered that a certain Simon de Manston,
who was in charge of the chapel at Sindlesham, was unable to
construe the mass. When asked what governed *Te* in *Te igitur
clementissime Pater*, he replied : 'Pater, for the Father governeth
all things'; and another young chaplain at Hurst remained perforce stubbornly silent as questions were put to him. Others followed suit, and the dean was obliged to suspend some of them
from office, while reprimanding quite a number for their illiteracy and insubordination. But not all chaplains were unlearned.
In 1522 one-sixth of all the unbeneficed clergy in London were
masters of art, a notable exception to the general rule.

John Mirk in his *Manuale Sacerdotus*, which was written in
the fourteenth century, dealt primarily with the duties and re-
sponsibilities of the humble priest, the medieval equivalent of
George Herbert's seventeenth-century country parson, warning
him indeed against the evils of ignorance and frivolity; but at
the same time roundly declaring that 'an unlearned but humble
priest is better than a learned but presumptuous one'. His two
sketches of the Good Priest and the Bad Priest were obviously
drawn from the unbeneficed clergyman. Of the good priest he
wrote :

The priest of God, whose soul is in his hands always, knows that
he is hired to celebrate every day . . . therefore he disposed himself to live soberly as to himself, justly as to the master he serves,
and piously towards God.

Yet he not only says his daily offices and celebrates mass regularly, but spends the rest of the day profitably by reading and study, hearing confessions, and after dinner engaging himself in 'honest manual work'. There is no suggestion that he should visit his parishioners regularly apart from the sick, but he must be careful to instruct them : advising the newly wed how to behave, telling parents how to bring up their children, briefing midwives how to carry out their duties, and impressing upon all his flock the necessity for reverence in church and churchyard, for the prompt payment of their tithes and for the avoidance of witchcraft and usury.

Contrariwise the bad priest is described as : 'Him we call the worldly priest, who loves the world, to be well fed, well clothed and to lead an easy life.' To this end he attaches himself to some wealthy patron and fawns upon him in the hope of a rich benefice :

On taking office he goes to the altar, not when devotion invites him, but when his lord insinuates; not out of devotion, but from habit; thinking nothing of Christ's passion, but only thinking how to prolong or shorten the mass to the will of his lord.

Old age, alas! does not improve him :

The bad old priest is garrulous, full of proverbs, and given to fables; sitting among his boon companions, he recites the wars of princes and instills into the ears of juniors anecdotes of his early life, which he ought to weep for rather than repeat.

In the thirteenth century the increasing importance of the mass, due to the doctrine of transubstantiation and the institution of the feast of Corpus Christi, led to the popularity of masses for the dead. Under medieval wills priests were hired for a period of one or more years to celebrate for the souls of the departed, a practice that vastly increased after the Black Death. Sometimes a will provided for an 'annual', i.e. a prescribed number of masses to be said each year for an indefinite period; but above all it was the perpetual chantry that enabled men and women of means to establish yet another pious institution akin to the founding of monasteries or colleges. These chantries normally came into existence during the patron's own life-time, so that its chaplain could offer up prayers and masses for the good estate of the founder and his relations in this world as well as the next. Generally speaking such a perpetual chantry was an endowed benefice, to which the chaplain was instituted and inducted, and whose duties were carefully prescribed and defined. Like a benefice too it gave him both security of tenure and an insured livelihood. But this was not always the case. It was possible to found a chantry where the priest received a fixed stipend from the trustees, but could be dismissed for a serious fault. What sort of priest undertook this kind of work? No doubt large numbers of needy chaplains made a living by celebrating as many of the special masses or 'annuals', provided for under wills, as possible. For this casual work they demanded the maximum income, especially after the Black Death when there was an extraordinary demand and priests were in short supply. Archbishop Islip roundly condemned their greed in 1362, declaring that they were 'drowned in an abyss of voluptuousness, costly apparel and shameless luxury, contrary to their vows and apostolic doctrine'. Legislation was ultimately introduced to limit the stipend to seven marks a year; but none of this applied to the perpetual chantries, which had their own endowments.

It has been suggested both by Langland and Chaucer that parish incumbents in large numbers forsook their cures for these rich sinecures. Langland wrote:

> Persones and Parishe prestes. pleynede to the bishop,
> That hure parshens ben poore. sitthe the pestelence tyme,
> To have licence and leue. in Londone to dwelle,
> And synge ther for symonye. for seluer ys swete.

And Chaucer's 'poure parson' denounced the priest who:

> Leet his sheep encombred in the myre,
> And ran to London unto Seynt Paules,
> To seken him a chaunterie for soules.

But in point of fact few rectors or vicars could obtain an episcopal licence to do so, except perhaps where chantries had been established in their own churches. Normally an unbeneficed priest of good repute was chosen, if possible some relation of the founder or a well-known local man, who was proficient in music, had a sound knowledge of latin, was good at accounts, and was prepared to regard the appointment as a whole-time job. Before he could be admitted he had to show his letters of orders and submit testimonials of good character; while on institution he took the oath of canonical obedience and swore to fulfil all the obligations of the foundation charter. Bishops insisted on an adequate endowment. Before the Black Death five marks per annum was considered sufficient; later it rose to six and many got as much as seven or even ten. But out of this income he had to provide himself with books and vestments, to attend to the upkeep of the lands and repair the buildings. He was expected to reside and perform the duties in person, although in times of sickness he might secure a substitute at his own expense, unless the chantry happened to be rich enough to support two chaplains, when he who was whole in body could shoulder the burdens of his incapacitated brother. In old age or incurable sickness, again if funds permitted, a chaplain could be retired on a pension of five or six marks. If no house was available the priest was expected to find lodgings near the church, and not, as has sometimes been supposed, live with the incumbent of the parish at the parsonage. Each chaplain had his clerk, 'instructed and of honest conduct', who helped him both in the celebration of the masses and also in the saying of the canonical hours. A furnished house was normally provided, but the chaplain had to buy his own food and clothing, the latter always to be of a sober and becoming nature. He usually employed other domestic servants besides his clerk, but women were not expected to live in. 'No woman,' it was often laid down in the foundation charter, 'shall in anywise dwell in the manse of the chantry, or serve the chaplains, except only when they are sick; but they may winnow corn and do other honest women's work there if the house needs it and withdraw as soon as it is done.' This did not of course prevent many chantry chaplains from keeping concubines *sub rosa*.

They were expected to be given to hospitality in so far as their limited funds permitted, but not to the extent of interfering with their duties. Guests, apart from the odd wayfarer, usually consisted of ecclesiastics and substantial laymen. Women were rigorously excluded. Regular holidays varied from a few days or weeks to several months in order to visit distant relations or go on a pilgrimage, provided always that the work of the chantry continued unabated. This was a good deal easier in a rich foundation containing two or more chaplains. At the Sponne chantry for instance a priest might once in a life-time visit Rome, which would involve a year's sabbatical leave, on condition that he caused the chantry to be served at his own expense during his absence.

Chaplains must normally have had a good deal of spare time on their hands once their regular ecclesiastical duties were completed, and this could be spent in looking after the property upon which the income depended, collecting rents, keeping accounts and even engaging in farming activities. The Fitz martin chantry at St. Lawrence, Lincoln, for example, which was founded in 1305, declared:

In order that each chaplain for the time being may be able the better to maintain the said chapel, and to till the said land with his own labour and at his own charges, I have given the said John the chaplain four horses of the price of forty shillings, one cart of the price of ten shillings, one plough with its gear of the price of four shillings, two harrows of the price of two shillings, and also sixty sheep of the price of two shillings each at the least, so that the same John may till the said land at his own charges, and each chaplain who succeeds him may cause it to be tilled likewise. And whenever the said chantry shall be vacant . . . the chaplain shall give up the horses, cart, plough, harrows and sheep or their price to his successors, together with a moiety of the corn both that which is sown and that which is growing on the land and which is in the grange.

The foundation deeds frequently laid it down that the chaplains must be learned men holding the university degree of M.A., B.D., or D.D. in order to be able to instruct youth. But this was by no means always the case. At the Dissolution of the chantries only some 200 priests out of 2,374 chantry chaplains were engaged in teaching. 'Teaching,' wrote A. G. Dickens in *The English Reformation*, 'was not indeed the normal duty of a chantry priest; in Shropshire about six out of fifty such priests conducted schools, in Yorkshire about thirty out of 400.'

Chantries could only be founded in parish churches with the consent of their incumbents, and it was always strictly enjoined in the founding deed that the chaplains were in no way to prejudice either his rights or those of his church by discouraging his people from paying their dues or 'to sow favour, or cause to be made dissensions, quarrels, or scandals between the said vicar and his parishioners'. He was further forbidden to perform any duty appertaining to the incumbent; but was expected to render voluntary help when required and to assist him in the saying of the daily offices. The chaplain's main occupation, of course, was the celebration of the masses specified in his foundation charter, which usually meant seven times a week. The mass said was the one for the day, but there were many exceptions as for example on saints' days or when he had to meet a special need such as a requiem. Yet whatever that mass might be the priest was obliged to offer up special prayers on behalf of the founder and his kin.

Despite all the safeguards there was sometimes friction between the incumbent and the chaplain over these masses, since it was found that parishioners took advantage of them as an excuse for not attending the parish celebration. In 1376 the bishop of Hereford forbade the chaplains at Ledbury to begin before the high mass, 'because when they celebrated earlier the parishioners attended their masses and then devoted the rest of the day to business and pleasure, to the neglect of high mass and other parochial duties'. But when the people attended the chantry masses they were expected to pray for the founder and his kin. The chaplain of Brydde's chantry at Marlborough parish church, for example, used to turn to the congregation at the first washing of his hands and say in English : 'For the soul of John Brydde and Isabel his wife my founders, and for all christian souls say you one Pater Noster and one Ave Maria.' Chaplains were also obliged to recite Pacebo, the office for the dead, the Dirgie, and the service of Commendation at least thrice during the week.

Chantry chaplains, like some parochial clergy, were often neglectful of their duties, irreverent in their performance, and sometimes immoral. For these and other offences they were rarely deprived, as trained singers, particularly after the Black Death, were hard to come by; so the usual punishment was either a fine or a penance. The latter was especially disliked. At Wells cathedral in 1490 John Pope, who was found guilty of adultery, was ordered by the dean : 'with bare head and feet, clad in his surplice, [he] should carry a wax candle of half a pound, before the procession in the church, and when the procession had entered the choir the said John was to stand in his stall, in the like form, until the end of mass saying the seven penitential psalms and at the time of the offertory he should offer the wax to St. Andrew.' John refused to comply, whereupon he was deprived, although subsequently restored. Among country chaplains, who had to cultivate their agricultural lands, the chief temptation was to say the canonical hours in the fields instead of wasting time by going home to the church.

Saxon nobles had usually installed a private chapel in their manors, which was served by a chaplain. The Norman conquerors continued the practice, and throughout the Middle Ages there was scarcely a castle in England that did not maintain one in its keep-tower. The largest was St. Peter ad Vincula in the Tower of London; and perhaps the finest in Hampton Court built by Cardinal Wolsey in the early sixteenth century. Oxford and Cambridge colleges together with schools like Eton and Winchester followed suit; while naturally all bishops possessed such chapels in their episcopal palaces. Medieval households were very large containing, besides a regular garrison of soldiers, a train of knights with their ladies, squires, yeomen, pages, grooms and serving men and women, while a constant flow of visitors passed through them. These provided an ample congregation. The clerical staff would consist at least of one chaplain with assistant clerks and some singing boys; but the more important nobles might employ very many more. The Earl of Northumberland at the beginning of the sixteenth century was served by a dean and ten other priests. These chaplains were of course completely subservient since their livelihood depended entirely upon the good will of their lord, who at his whim could find them rich benefices or turn them adrift to seek their bread. 'Nor,' wrote John Mirk, 'does the priest only strive to please his lord whom he serves, but also the whole household, so that at the opportune time, when any church falls vacant, of which his lord is the patron, then they also would put in a good word for him to the lord.'

Despite canonical prohibitions chaplains were normally expected to undertake secular work as well as their religious duties; to act as steward, secretary or tutor. When the lord owned the advowsons of surrounding villages the castle chapel could well become the mother church of the neighbourhood, whose churches would be served by the domestic chaplains. Castle chapels were consecrated and under the jurisdiction of the bishop, who licensed them for divine worship. There must have been nearly 7,000 of them in England and Wales. It was stipulated, however, that their congregations must attend their parish churches on Sundays and festivals; and all dues, fees, offerings, etc., given to the parish priest and not to the chaplain, who was paid directly by his lord, ate at his table and lodged in his castle or manor house. These chapels were occasionally licensed for marriages and might be very sumptuously furnished with several altars, beautiful hangings, service books, vestments and perhaps even an organ. The services themselves consisted of mattins and mass before breakfast, and evensong before dinner. The former were cut down to the bare essentials on hunting days, being known as 'hunting masses'. It was possible for well-to-do yeomen or citizens to employ domestic chaplains; although this did not occur very frequently. So, in all, this form of ecclesiastical service catered for large numbers of unbeneficed priests.

CHAPTER III

The Reformation and After

Immediately prior to the Reformation the number of curates and chantry priests was very large indeed; the former an exploited group upon whom the parochial system, especially in the country, principally depended. Their average income varied between £5 and £3 or less, and since they usually had no glebe it was not easy for them to supplement their earnings in other ways. Yet strangely enough the abolition of the monastic houses, followed by that of the chantries and then in 1550 of all minor orders, which saw a clerical proletariat numbering many thousands disappear into the ranks of the laity, did not occasion the upheaval in the Church's structure that might have been expected. No decline in spirituality or morality was noticeable, while by the end of the sixteenth century higher standards of parochial administration were being provided by the clergy than ever before, particularly in the fields of instruction and preaching. On the other hand many of them were worse off financially, especially curates and poor vicars who possessed no glebe and lived on small fixed incomes that were being rapidly corroded by inflation. The scope of clerical employment was also drastically reduced, since from the time that the Reformation really began to take effect until after the Restoration curates were rarely employed to assist resident incumbents, unless the latter were old or infirm, but were almost exclusively used either to supply parishes where the rector or vicar was non-resident, or else to serve impropriations and chapels of ease. This indeed was a far cry from the Middle Ages when large clerical staffs were the order of the day in most livings.

Under the Pluralities Act of 1529 double-beneficed men were required to reside upon 'one at least of their livings'; and by the canons of 1583, 1597 and 1604 they were expected to live in each of them 'for some reasonable time in every year'; but were obliged to supply a curate to perform the duties during their absence. The Pluralities Act indeed demanded that the bishops themselves should be charged with the task of seeing that these curates were safely installed into such cures and were provided with an adequate income under the episcopal seal. It declared :

The cure of the church be in the meanwhile well supplied in all things by some fit minister, able to explain and interpret the Principles of the Christian Religion, and to preach the Word of God to the People; and if the revenues of the said church can conveniently maintain such an one. And that a competent and sufficient salary for this purpose be limited and appointed by the Bishop of the place or (in case the diocesan bishop do not do his duty herein) by the Archbishop or his successor, to be given and paid bona fide to the said curate.

Also under the First Fruits (Restitution to Next Incumbent) Act of 1536, the curate, who was appointed by the sequestrators to administer a vacant benefice, must receive the whole of the income; but if that income was not sufficient for his needs he could recover the difference from the next incumbent. These statutes were later reinforced by the 1604 canons, although they were never actually sanctioned by Parliament. 'Every beneficed man,' reiterated Canon 47, 'licensed by the laws of the realm, upon urgent occasions of other service, not to reside upon his benefice, shall cause his cure to be supplied by a curate that is a sufficient and licensed preacher, if the worth of the benefice will bear it. But whosoever hath two benefices shall maintain a preacher, licensed in the benefice where he doth not reside, except he preach himself at both of them usually.' In practice, however, few of these curates were at first sufficiently learned to be licensed to preach, and had to content themselves with reading the authorised homilies and catechising, while importing licensed preachers from outside the parish to give those monthly sermons that were demanded by canon 46. Furthermore curates were not expected

to serve more than one church per Sunday, 'except that a chapel
be a member of the Parish Church or united thereunto, and
unless the said church or chapel, where such a minister shall
serve in two places, be not able in the judgement of the Bishop
or Ordinary to maintain a curate'. High educational and pastoral
standards were demanded from all curates. 'No bishop,' declared
canon 34, 'shall henceforth admit any person into sacred
orders . . . except he be either of one of the universities of this
realm . . . and hath taken some degree of school of either of the
said universities; or at the least, except he be able to yield an
account of his faith in latin . . . and to confirm the same by sufficient testimonials out of the holy scriptures.' Then whatever their
'qualities and gifts' no candidate for holy orders might be ordained
deacon and priest on the same day, since it was essential that
'there may ever be some kind of trial of their behaviour in the
office of deacon, before they be admitted to the order of the
priesthood'. Finally it was laid down that no one should be
ordained without a valid title, either to a cure of souls, a chaplaincy, a fellowship, or 'except he be a Master of Arts of five
years' standing, that liveth of his own charge in either of the
universities.'

But at first such ideals were unattainable, since the Reformation by reducing both the prestige and status of the clergy *vis-
à-vis* the laity led to an alarming decline in their numbers from
Edward VI's reign onwards. Indeed, immediately prior to the
introduction of the new English Ordinal in March 1549–50
ordinations almost dried up completely, which was probably
mainly due to disapproval of the new Protestantism. But under
the Ordinal itself some 116 men received holy orders, most of
whom either went into exile during Mary's reign and did not
return until after her death, were deprived in the early months of
1553–4 because they were married, or suffered death by burning
for their faith; although there was never any official attempt to
make Edwardine orders a pretext for deprivation. On the contrary they were recognised not only as qualifying a man to remain

1.　Wooden church in Greensted, Essex, built A.D. 1013.

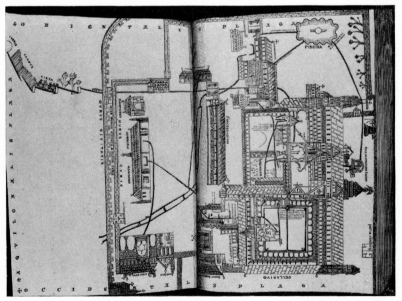

2.　Plan of Canterbury cathedral church and monastery; from a manuscript c. 1130.

3.   Medieval rectory in Northamptonshire.

4.   The private chapel at Haddon Hall, Derbyshire.

6. Confiscation of relics and treasure during the Dissolution of the Monasteries.

5. De-La-Warr Chantry, Boxgrove, Sussex.

7. Preaching in the open air *c.* 1576.

8. A would-be pluralist incumbent
requiring 'a curate on easy terms'.

in his curacy, but also for promotion to a benefice; especially in view of the fact that these Edwardian clergy were of a higher educational standard than either the Marian or early Elizabethan ordinands.

It is worth recording the story of one of these Edwardian curates, who suffered martyrdom, George Marsh, who was curate and schoolmaster at Allhallows in Bread Street, London, under an incumbent and fellow-martyr named Laurence Saunders. He fled to Lancashire on the outbreak of the Marian persecution, where, according to Foxe, 'he continued for a space earnestly setting forth God's true religion, to the decaying of anti-christ's false doctrine, by his godly readings and sermons'. Here he was arrested in March 1555, charged before the Earl of Derby and Bishop of Chester, and condemned to death by burning. 'The earl asked me,' he recorded, 'whether I was a priest. I said no. Then he asked me what had been my living. I answered I was a minister, served a cure and taught a school. Then said my lord to his council, This is a wonderful thing : afore he said he was no priest, and now he confesseth himself to be one. I answered, By the laws now used in this realm, as far as I know, I am none. Then they asked me who gave me Orders or whether I had taken any at all. I answered, I received Orders of the Bishops of London and Lincoln. Then said they, one to another, Those be of these new heretics. . . . They asked me how long I had been curate, and whether I had ministered with a good conscience. I answered, I had been curate but one year, and had ministered with a good conscience, I thanked God : and if the laws of the realm would have suffered me I would have ministered still, and if the law at anytime hereafter would suffer me to minister after that sort I would minister again.'

Evidently his judges did not question the authenticity of Marsh's orders; but he himself repudiated the title of priest because the Marian laws, which he could not accept having originally taken oaths against the Papal jurisdiction, refused to allow him to officiate as such.

Religious persecution and deprivation had sadly reduced the number of the parochial clergy by the beginning of Elizabeth's reign; and suitable candidates were slow in coming forward. They were discouraged for financial reasons, since in this respect the Church was not so attractive as the medical or legal professions. Consequently as many as 2,000 of the poorer benefices remained vacant, and in order to fill the gaps the Elizabethan bishops were compelled to lower their educational standards and admit men of mean mental capacity and low social status. Archbishop Parker confessed to Bishop Grindal of London in 1560: 'Whereas, occasioned by the great want of ministers we and you both, for tolerable supply thereof, have heretofore admitted into the ministry sundry artificers and others, not traded and brought up in learning, and, as it happened in a multitude some that were of base occupations'.

The Lincoln ordination lists between 1555 and 1585 go to prove that many non-graduate clergy were drawn from such base callings as day-labourers, serving men, ostlers, husbandmen, carpenters, glovers, drapers, tallow chandlers, shoemakers, soldiers, clothiers, etc.; and other diocesan records of this period show that many bishops were ordaining men of similar occupations. It was rare throughout the sixteenth century for a curate to have a degree. In the Worcester diocese, for example, none of the sixty curates licensed between 1579 and 1584 were graduates; the visitation call books of the archdeaconry of Oxford from 1576 to 1586 show that almost all the curates in this area were referred to as 'domini' not 'magistri'; and Archdeacon Powell's return to Archbishop Parker of the state of the Gloucester diocese in 1561 mentions only three curate graduates, who had risen to four by 1592–3.

On the other hand it was unlikely that many of them were totally illiterate. The churchwardens at Woodchester, Gloucestershire, indeed suggested in 1563 that their curate could not write: 'The Register of christenings, burialls and mariages,' they complained, 'hath not ben well kept by the default of one sir John

Randall who was curat under Mr. Wye who could not write to make the boke perfyte'; and others were accused of not being able to read distinctly. 'We have,' declared the churchwardens of Eastington in the same county and at the same date, 'no curate but an ould man which ys not able to read distinctly and perfectly as he ought to do.' The curate of Lower Swell also could not 'say service', but only because 'he is impotent and blinde'; and another of Coughton and Studley in Warwickshire during 1586 was unable to read English properly on account of being 'one Robert Cathell, a seelie Welshman'. But more was expected from curates than just being able to read and write. If they had no degree they should at least have been to one of the many grammar schools, which were now springing up in most parts of the country and were open to all boys of ability, where they would learn fluent latin and a thorough knowledge of the Scriptures. Alas, this was often far from the case. In the Liber Cleri of 1576, which recorded the bishop of Lincoln's visitation of the Leicester, Lincoln and Stowe archdeaconries, it was noted that only 167 clergy were latinists, 207 'sufficiently qualified in sacred learning', 226 'ignorant' and 206 'deficient in any sort of knowledge'. Many were described as 'utterlie ignorant'. Most of these last were curates. Earlier in 1551 Bishop Hooper of Gloucester found ten curates unable to repeat the Lord's Prayer, and a large number of others who could not say the Ten Commandments.

Strenuous attempts were made to improve the position both before and after ordination. A declaration of 1562 decreed that no bishop should admit anyone into holy orders 'who is not learned, fit to teach the people'; and in order to ensure these higher educational standards they must be prepared to accept pluralism as the price and restrict the entry of ill-educated ordinands. At Archbishop Cranmer's prompting an Act of Parliament had been passed in 1539, 31 Henry VIII c. 9., which was designed to make the cathedrals nurseries of the clergy. 'He had projected,' wrote Gilbert Burnet in his *History of the Reformation*, 'that in every cathedral there should be provision made for readers in divinity, and of Greek and Hebrew; and a great number of students to be both exercised in the daily worship of God and trained up in study and devotion, whom the bishop might transplant out of the nursery into all parts of his diocese. And thus every bishop should have had a college of clergymen under his eyes.'

This scheme bore little fruit; but the great increase in secondary education during the second half of the century, together with a remarkable revival of learning at the universities, gradually made their influence felt and enabled many men of plebeian origin to enter the Church adequately equipped. There was also an intensive drive to educate them *after* ordination. Some bishops, indeed, refused either to priest deacons or institute curates to livings until they had prosecuted their studies more deeply. When Robert Andrews, curate of Market Harborough, presented himself to be priested in 1573 Bishop Cooper of Lincoln 'enjoined him to forbeare taverne and ale house in all places whatsoever and to increase his knowledge in the Latin tongue'; but accepted John Leech, curate of Northill, Bedfordshire, who 'appeared and satisfied the bishop, with his study'. Another candidate, Thomas Morley, was ordained priest 'upon necessitye, although in the holy scriptures unacquainted', but he did not receive his letters of orders until he had shown he had profited by a study of the Bible. The same Morley, when three years later he was presented to the rectory of Wyberton, was refused institution since on examination the bishop still found him to be ignorant. He was told 'to apply his study' for six months, and on again failing to satisfy the bishop had the mortification of seeing his rectory bestowed upon another. A year later he was instituted to the vicarage of Heckington. Archbishop Grindal of York also declined to institute nine of his clergy on account of their insufficient learning, including one curate who thought that the Israelites were led out of Egypt by King Saul.

The Royal Injunctions of 1559 and Archbishop Parker's Advertisements of 1566 had directed the bishops and archdeacons to examine all their clergy below the degree of M.A. at their visitations to find out 'how they have profited in the Study of the Holy Scripture'; and in particular, 'to appoint curates to certain taxes of the New Testament to be conned without book, and at the next synod enact a rehearsal of them', an injunction to be repeated in the canons of 1571. It may not have been practical in the sixteenth century for all the clergy to have degrees, to be latinists, or possess the ability to preach, but at least it should not be asking the impossible to demand a competent knowledge of the Scriptures. In his injunctions of 1577 Bishop Cooper of Lincoln declared that ministers should 'bend themselves diligently to the study of the holy Scriptures and Word of God . . . every day in the week . . . to read over one chapter at least of the Bible, taking some notes in a paper book of such wholesome sentences and good matter as he shall observe in the reading of the Bible as *The Decades* [i.e. Bullinger's *Decades*] . . . that he may show the same when he shall be thereunto called'. Other bishops followed suit, concentrating on such a study rather than Greek or latin; and out of many examples we may quote the general exhortation of Archbishop Grindal of York to the clergy of his Northern Province in 1571 :

Ye shall daylie reade at least one chapter of the oulde Testament and another of the New with good advisement, and such of you as be under the degree of a maister of arts shall provide and have of your owne, according to the quenes majesties injunctions, at least the New Testament both in latine and English, conferringe the one with the other everye day one chapter thereof at the leaste, so upon examination of the Archdeacon comissary or their officers in synodes and visitations or at other appointed tymes it may appeare ye profit in the studye of holy scripture.

In Essex the archdeacon of Colchester demanded at his visitation of 1586 that his clergy should buy certain theological books, pursue a definite course of theological study and compose specimen sermons under the supervision of special tutors appointed by himself. Curates in particular were often expected to learn from other clergy better qualified than themselves. Valentine Blake, curate of Winchcombe in Gloucestershire, for example, was referred by the bishop to a certain Mr. Jenkins, who was schoolmaster there, for this purpose. With the result that the clergy as a whole during the last two decades of Elizabeth's reign were probably better educated than they had ever been. Not unnaturally the poor curates remained the least satisfactory both in social status and academic learning; yet as the returns of the archbishop of York's chaplains, who had been sent to conduct a special visitation of the clergy in 1580, show, they were generally zealous and honest if not always very intelligent or well-educated. For instance, Jacob Foster, the sixty-six year old curate of Giggleswick, is described as hardworking, but only moderately acquainted with the sacred Scriptures; another, William Taylor, curate of Scarborough, knew his Bible, was diligent and religious, and catechised the ignorant; a third, Thomas Masterman, curate of Dighton, knew no latin, but was honest, zealous and diligent; a fourth, Robert Henrison, the Scotch curate of Lockington, knew little latin, but studied hard and was a man of unblameable life; finally out of many others there was Richard Gill the seventy-two year old curate of Thornton, who is described as *vir honestus et zelosus*.

Yet however ill-educated, the curate was expected to teach in his parish school; although as a rule he would be 'dumb' in the sense of not being licensed to preach. 'In what parish church or chapel soever,' runs canon 78 (1604), 'there is a curate, which is a Master of Arts, or Bachelor of Arts, or is otherwise well able to teach youth, and will willingly do so, for the better increase of his living, and training up children in the principles of true religion; we will and ordain that a licence to teach youth of the parish where he serveth be granted to none by the Ordinary of that place, but only to the said curate. Provided always, that this Constitution shall not extend to any parish or chapel in the country towns, where there is a public school founded already; in which case we think it not meet to allow any to teach grammar but only him that is allowed for the said public school.' At Sutton in Essex Margaret Shipden was presented by the churchwardens 'for teaching of a school, whereas our Curate who is allowed by my Lord Bishop is willing and desirous to do the same for the more increasing of his living'. The same criticism applied to Nicholas Cole and his daughter at West Wittering in Sussex, who, unlicensed, were luring children away from another curate, 'who, being licensed to teach, doth gladly take paynes to teach children and to bring them up in good letters and for the better mayntenance of himself'. Certainly most curates were in need of a 'better mayntenance', since their stipends increased only very slowly during this period. In answer to Bishop Freake of Worcester's visitation articles of 1585 twenty-three curates replied to his question about their salaries as follows: one curate received £12 per annum, four earned £10 and the remaining eighteen were paid £8 10s. or less. The worst of all was the curate of Shelsley Beauchamp who had 'no more but only 30s. by yeare for his wages over and above the casuall profytes of the church that ys worth above 7s. by the yeare'. Curates' stipends in the Lincoln diocese at the beginning of the seventeenth century were no better. In 1603 forty-six of them were being paid £5, sixty-four £10, twenty-one £15, eleven £20, and one was fortunate enough to obtain £36. Even as late as 1650 the wealthy rector of Fladbury, Worcestershire, who drew an income of £600 from his benefice, gave his curate at Bradley £10, another at Wyre Piddle £8, and a third at Throckmorton £6, plus some small tithes. On an average then the Elizabethan curate could expect to earn anything from £10 to £5 or less. Agricultural labourers were better off. Some indeed served for a mere pittance. During the first two decades of Elizabeth's reign small ill-endowed livings were often served by wandering ministers, who prowled 'up and down like masterless hounds, being glad to serve . . . for a piece of silver and a morsel of bread.' Archbishop Bancroft referred in 1605 to curates, 'who are content to serve for ten groats a year and a canvas doublet'. Two years later

55

an Essex curate was receiving only £5 6s. 8d. and 'his diet'.

But there was always the hope, however faint, of eventually graduating to a fat rectory, where, with the rapidly rising price of corn, the value of the greater tithes was soaring. In the meantime they could and did supplement their income in other ways. The most satisfactory were either to teach for fees, secure an appointment to one of the endowed lectureships that were springing up in most townships, or act as chaplain to one of the gentry—the last of which entailed the indignity of being classed by their master with his domestic servants. But they could also engage in secular employments, for which perhaps some of them had been qualified by their pre-ordination occupations. This would not in any way detract from the respect accorded them by their parishioners, who were accustomed anyway to see their parson working as a farmer six days in the week. Such activities included sheep and cattle-breeding, weaving, and even money-lending or keeping the village inn. Richard Baxter as a boy was acquainted with two 'poor ignorant curates', one of whom cut faggots and the other made ropes. Occasionally a pluralist would lease out one of his livings to his curate at an easy rent, while the profits the latter made would be in lieu of salary. In reply to Bishop Freake's visitation articles of 1585 the curate of Morton Bagot estimated that he obtained an income of £6 per annum by farming the living from his non-resident rector; and the curate of Aston Cantlow made £10 a year in the same way.

The puritans in particular approved of this combination of the sacred and the secular, judging from the following 'humble supplication' to the Queen in 1584 :

> The bishops forthwith ask, what shall our curates do,
> Or what allowance shall they have to live upon?
> We say we think it best that out of hand they go
> To their old trades or learn some occupation.
> Then did they storm with angry mood, saying that we
> Would have all vicars through the land beggars to be.

On the other hand the puritans did not approve of pluralities, where non-resident incumbents employed non-preaching curates, whom they dubbed 'dumb' and 'blynd'. Puritan surveys covering nine English counties in 1586 showed that there were some 565 incumbents occupying 1,933 livings, where less than one in four was providing a preaching minister. Furthermore they estimated in 1603 that a thousand pluralists held between them 2,500 benefices, of which one in every six was served by a 'dumb' curate. A paper in the Lincoln Registry dated 1605 gives a number of examples : 'Mr. Griffin parson of Litell Ponton and Kirby Underwood, and a blynd curat serves one of them; Mr. Williams parson of Asgarby and Aswarby, and a blynd curat serves one of them; Mr. Gaze vicar of Hunington and Ancaster, a blynd curat serves one of them.' Such men could hardly expect more than a few pounds a year, since, poor scholars as they were, their services both for preaching and teaching would be negligible, and were largely confined to celebrating the sacraments, saying the offices, reading the homilies and taking the occasional services. The bishops did their best to keep pluralities within limits; and under the canons of 1571 incumbents were forbidden to hold more than two benefices at once, which had to be within twenty-six miles of one another. The 1604 canons extended the distance to thirty miles, but insisted that an adequately educated curate should be installed into any living where the incumbent was non-resident. By 1640 one clergyman in every five was a pluralist and hence an employer of curates, whose qualifications however were now very much better and not even the puritans could term them 'dumb' or 'blynd'. In the Oxford diocese, for example, the curates of the 1630s were a very highly educated group of men. Of the forty-six who were licensed to curacies between May 1631 and October 1635 all except one described themselves either as a master or bachelor of arts. During Elizabeth's reign curates were continually moving from one parish to another in order to try and better themselves. In the short period between 1579 and 1585 seven livings in the Worcester diocese had more than one change of curate. But by the middle of the next century men were serving cures for much longer periods.

Pluralism then flourished on the three-fold argument that the endowments of most parishes were too small to support a parson, there was a shortage of clergy, and high educational standards must be maintained at any cost. All attempts to abolish it, and there were many, proved futile. Archbishop Whitgift in his *Defence of the Answer to the Admonition* championed non-residence against the puritans on the grounds of necessity : 'No one "watchman",' he said, 'is continually in the tower, neither is it possible that he should be : it is sufficient if the tower be watched, and the chief watch man neglect not his duty. "The Shepherd" also is not always present with his sheep, but sometime he leaveth them alone, when he hath folded them, or brought them into a safe pasture, and sometimes he committeth them to his "servant" or some other "to be kept in his obedience".'

Elizabethan episcopal visitation returns disclose the unsatisfactory nature and many failings of some of these curate 'servants'. In 1597 James Manninge, curate of Boughton, Norfolk, was presented because 'he seldome or never weareth the surples, and seldom readeth the Comination of synners. He is a Common gamester at unlawful games. . . . He doth not catechise. He hath and doth use to plowge, harrowe and cart as a layman . . . he playethe at cards.' The rubric at the end of 1559 Confirmation Service had directed that 'the Curate of every parish, or some other at his appointment, shall diligently upon Sundays and holy days, half an hour before Evening Prayer, openly in the Church instruct and examine so many children of his parish sent unto him, as the time will serve as he shall think convenient, in some part of the Catechism'. This rubric many curates failed to observe; notably a certain Mr. Cooke, curate of West Bilney in 1597, of whom we are told : 'he doth not instructe the yowth on Sundayes and holidayes. . . . He receaveth to the Communion those which have not bene Confirmed.' The same failure to catechise was found in the case of three contemporary curates at

Ipswich : John Wakelyn of St. Lawrence, who 'catechiseth not the youth by reason he preacheth everie Saboth daie'; John Glozinge of St. Margaret's, who 'dothe not instructe the youthe in the Catechism . . . he declareth not what holidaies or fastinge daies in the weeke following'; and John Sheton of St. Mary-le-Tower, who 'doth not catachise the youth uppon Saboth and holydaies because they have daylie sermons twice everie Sabbothe daies'. None of these gentlemen wore the surplice, they neglected the perambulations, left out parts of the Prayer Book services, and omitted their Wednesday and Friday duties. They were evidently fanatical puritans, who much preferred the dangerous art of preaching the Word, even though unlicensed to do so, to the more humdrum tasks of reading the homilies and catechising.

Another East Anglian curate, William Wells of St. George's, Colegate, Norfolk, was addicted to the sin of irregular baptisms. 'A bason,' it was alleged, 'is sett onto the font in the tyme of baptisme.' Others like Mr. Waddisworth of Dunston read the services 'at unseasonable hours'. The Yorkshire curates were no better. At Cherry-Burton in 1575 it was said : 'Thomas Davye ther Curate doth not reade the threatninge against synners in their churche naither doth he teache the youthe of their parishe the Catechisme'. Thomas Hingeston, curate of St. Crux, York, was accused in 1598 of 'ministering communion to an excommunicate person'; while at Walley in Lancashire a couple were married without banns in 'a parlor or chamber within the dwelling house of Sir Miles Caryer of Downeham Chapell'. Others were charged with reading the services inaudibly, of refusing to catechise the young even when 'wayges offered for it,' of expounding the Scriptures instead of reading the homilies, of not 'using the perambulations' and neglecting to wear the surplice. But perhaps the worst offence of all was to continue to practice the so-called superstitions of the Old Faith. Henry Laughe, curate of Bridlington, for instance, went on administering the wafer against the express command of 'the quenes auctority'; Thomas Briggs, curate of Pateley Bridge, another reputed papist, went so far as to try and 'seduce others by his synister whisperinge in their eares'; and at Prescot in 1568 it was reported that: 'Sir Rauf Nunt curate . . . usethe to make holly water . . . goying about with the same to blesse people and beastes'.

One of the curates of Ripon Minster, who had conducted services and churched women in one of the disused saints' chapels, had to make the following public confession:

. . . drawinge by my lewd example other from that place (the choir) to the said Lady Lofte where of old tyme idolytry and damnable supersticious worshippings have been usually frequented to the perill and daunger not only of myne owne sowle but of those whome I have misled, I am now hartelie sory. . . . And also for that I unto whome the chardge of the fabrick of this churche is committed have hitherto suffered the old abhominable and supersticious vawte called Wilfredes Nedle and alter therein and certain other altares also to remain hitherto unto within this churche undefaced undestroyed and not tayken away contrary to the lawes of this realme and my dewty and to the great daunger of my soule. And I besiche you all to pray with me.

Curates were not supposed to serve more than one cure at a time, although some of the bishops allowed them, in consideration of their poverty, to act as private chaplains to the gentry, provided they always used the Prayer Book services. The unsatisfactory Mr. Cooke, for instance, was rapped over the knuckles because in addition to West Bilney, 'he serveth Pentnye allso'. But when Hugh Richards, curate of Goring in Oxfordshire, was reprimanded for doing duty at Basildon in Berkshire, he replied that he did so 'at the requeste of Master Davies vicare of Basseldesne whoe hath beene troobled this long tyme with matters of lawe or sickness soe he coulde not intend his owne cure and churche'. He admitted that he also needed the cash, but vehemently insisted that he always so arranged matters that 'the service is doone in both places in good convenient tyme daylie'.

Some curates, alas, were notorious for their unseemly conduct: Robert Hiat, curate of Bampton, Oxfordshire, was a particularly bad offender. Returning home one Friday evening the worse for drink in the company of a fellow curate, Richard Palmer of Brize Norton, and one of his own parishioners, William Woodward, he and the last named gentleman exchanged words and then blows. 'Upon occasion of evill woordes utered bye ye sayde Sr Hiate against this respondent,' Woodward later testified before the archdeacon's court, 'this respondent gave him a blowe wth a smale coogell over the back and used no other violence against him and sorie for that he hathe doone it.' The same year, 1584, Hiat was alleged to have fathered an illegitimate child upon a girl named Jane Pusie. William Cooke of Sandford alleged: 'that about Candlemas last one Robert Hiat curate of Bampton did bringe into this respondentes howse the articulate Jane Pusie beinge great wth child and promised that this respondent should have Xs for a moneth, and that they wold discharge him this respondent againste the courte, and saith further that he kepith the child still and that he should have of the said Mr. Hiat XIId a weeke for keeping the said child.' Hiat's friend and boon-companion, Richard Palmer, was equally reprehensible. He admitted *'carnalem copulam cum Dorothea Maye de Bampton'*, and also *'cum Martha Joanes'*, who was the wife of John Joanes, one of his parishioners at Brize Norton. Another notorious case was that of a neighbouring curate, Henry Wise of Horton, who was accused of incontinency, brawling, tavern-haunting and gambling. He denied them all and was dismissed with an admonition. He indeed declared on oath that he did not 'haunt evill companie of women' and 'that he is not a quareler nor table player other than wth honest gentlemen, and at honest and convenient tymes; he is no dice player nor doth use any rybald talke . . . that one Hawle did disturb him in his service and therupon he willed the churchwardens to carie him owt of the churche, and otherwise he did not brawle'. It would seem that he did protest too much!

Some of the northern curates were no better: Robert Clough, curate of Kirby Chapel, was reputed to be 'a sorcerer, a hawker and a hunter', and was severely admonished by the Bishop of Chester. Tristram Tildesley, curate of Rufford in Lancashire, became notorious in his district as a buffoon. In 1581 'not having the feare of God before his eyes . . . upon Sondaies and hollidaies hath daunced emongst light and youthful companie both men and women at weddings drynkings and rush bearings . . . did daunce skip leape emongest a great multitude of people wher he was deryded flowted and laughed at'. Moreover instead of wearing 'decent apparrell and sware cap lyke a minister of his vocation', he 'hath worne and had most comonlye a long sword and round cloke'. The indictment ended with the complaint that he was 'a common haunter and user of aylehouses and a common player at unlawfull games in unlawful tymes and places'.

Such failings, combined often with a grinding poverty, little learning and a low social status, aroused the contempt and sometimes the active anti-clericalism of the laity. To lead an Elizabethan curate astray and then denounce him to the ecclesiastical authorities became in some parishes a recognised sport among the more undesirable elements of his congregation. But not all curates were poor, illiterate, down-trodden or morally unsatisfactory. Robert Parkyn, curate of Adwick-le-Street in Yorkshire, for example, was a learned man and a well-known writer, who had inherited a family estate, the rents of which were a welcome addition to his meagre stipend of £6 a year. His brother, a Fellow of Trinity College, Cambridge, used to send him parcels of books by the carrier. Such a minister was greatly respected and looked up to by his flock; and he did much good in his locality. Sometimes too it was not the curate but his employer who was the dullard. Edmund Pepper, curate of Bainton also in Yorkshire, denounced his rector, Marmaduke Atkinson, before the archbishop's court for illiteracy. He was unable, or so Pepper alleged, to find the gospel for the day, read *nobis* for *vobis* and 'sounded the accusative case for the ablative case and one case for another'.

Something remains to be said about clerical marriage. In Henry VIII's reign an attempt had been made to secure for the secular clergy the right to marry; but the king had frowned upon the notion, and even went so far as to issue a proclamation on 16 November 1521 threatening married clergy with deprivation and imprisonment. However, in 1549 Convocation sanctioned the marriage of priests, and this permission was confirmed by Parliament two years later. The Edwardine clergy in large numbers took full advantage of the concession, only to see this Act repealed under Mary's great Statute of Repeals in 1553, when the queen also issued a proclamation inhibiting the married clergy from administering or saying mass. The deprivations followed immediately numbering roughly one in every six incumbents, and two unbeneficed clergymen for every five who were beneficed. The queen's injunctions of 4 March 1553–4 instructed the bishops to remove immediately 'all such persons from their benefices and ecclesiastical promotions who contrary to the state of their order and the laudable custom of the church have married and used women as their wives, or otherwise notably and slaunderously disordered or abused themselves, sequestering also during the said process the fruits and profits of the said benefices and ecclesiastical promotions'. But after deprivation restitution was possible under certain conditions. For the queen's letter went on to declare : 'that when a priest separated from his wife and had done penance, the bishop might readmit him to officiate so it be not in the same place'. Edmund Alstone, for example, who was curate at St. Mary's-at-Hill in London, was stated in Bishop Bonner's register for 1554 to have performed his penance satisfactorily, given assurances for the future, and hence had been absolved from ecclesiastical censures and admitted to officiate in another parish; one of the reasons given for his reinstatement being that priests were now in short supply. John Browne, curate of 'Wymbaldowne', was likewise restored to the ministry, although in his case the offence had been aggravated by the marriage of two wives in succession. On the other hand John Elyot, clerical schoolmaster and curate of St. Leonard's, Eastcheap, who described his occupation as 'teaching petits their English prymers, catachysmes, and such like English books', and had married Joane Baile, by whom there were several children, was not deprived at all. He agreed to separate from his wife and in future to teach latin only.

With Elizabeth's accession to the throne the parson's wife came creeping back again, although the queen never really approved of her; and it was not until 1604 that she was once again recognised by law. The Royal Injunctions of 1559 laid down some strict rules concerning clerical matrimony, which were rigorously enforced. 'It is thought . . . very necessary,' they demanded, 'that no manner of priest or deacon shall hereafter take to his wife any manner of woman without the advice and allowance first upon good examination of the bishop of the diocese, and two justices of the peace of the same shire'. But these regulations were not always complied with. William Coxson, curate of Benson in Oxfordshire, was cited to the court of the Peculiar of Dorchester, presided over by the archdeacon of Oxford's official on 21 February 1591–2, for having married in irregular circumstances. His banns had only been read twice, and he confessed : 'he had not the handes of two justices of peace concerninge her good Conversacion accordinge to the statute in yt behalfe provyded, nether had he the consent of the Ordinarie thereunto'. William Hutchinson, curate of Felmersham in Bedfordshire was in even worse case, since he had been presented in June 1576, 'touchinge his marryeing two wyves'. Marrying and keeping a wife could prove an expensive matter, especially for a poor curate; and as so often happens the poorer they were the larger their families. Hence we find such curates eagerly looking round for ways and means of improving their income in any manner open to them. They usually had no glebe, so the most promising field lay in teaching for fees, particularly as a curate possessed the legal right to a monopoly of schoolmastering in his own parish. At first clerical marriage was unpopular in the country at large, since it was felt that it might destroy the ritual purity upon which the efficacy of the sacraments depended, that the children of the parsonage would

The Carefull
RESIDENT.

The Carelefs
NON‑RESIDENT.

9.   Satire on pluralities; from a seventeenth century tract.

10. Stephen Hale. 1677–1761.
Perpetual Curate of Teddington.

11. An eighteenth-century country curate.

12.   Satire on the high standard of living of clergymen 1741.

13.   The Old Clergy House, Alfriston, Sussex.

14. Satire on the self-indulgent clergy 1773.

15. A country curate *c.* 1793.

increase an already overlarge population and add to the scramble
for jobs, and that the parson himself would increase his financial
demands upon his parishioners. In 1610 at King's Sutton, Northamptonshire, a certain Hugo Holland and his wife Deanes were
reported to have said, 'the World was never merrie since preasts
wear married'; and further remarked of their own curate's wife,
Mrs. Smith, 'the first night she was married to him gave hir selffe
to the divell'. However, the parson's wife had arrived to stay,
very soon prejudice died away, and by the middle of the seventeenth century she had come to be regarded as an indispensable
part of village life.

E

CHAPTER IV

The Seventeenth-Century Curate

By the beginning of the seventeenth century clerical educational standards were rising sharply and showed a marked improvement upon those of the Elizabethan age. In 1585, for example, only 399 out of the 1,085 clergy in the Lincoln diocese were graduates; but by 1603 this number had increased to 646. Between 1617 and 1637 the annual recipients of Cambridge B.A. degrees were in the region of 266 of whom about 207 were regularly ordained; while at the sister university of Oxford over the same period some 172 graduates took holy orders yearly. This annual intake of 379 graduate ordinands was about sufficient to fill most of the vacant livings; although they sometimes scorned to supply the very poor ones, which continued to be served by low-grade ministers. Sir Benjamin Rudyer said in the House of Commons during 1628: 'There were then (1625) as now many accusations on foot against scandalous ministers: I was bold to tell the House that there were scandalous livings too, which were much the cause of the other. Livings five marks and five pounds a year; that men of worth and of good parts would not be muzzled up to such pittances.' Indeed by the 1630s the number of graduate ordinands was so large that it was not always easy to find them titles, and bishops were sometimes obliged to reject them. John Bancroft, bishop of Oxford, for instance, refused to ordain all the graduates who came to him; and Sir Thomas Wyatt, rector of Ducklington, tells us in his diary of the sad story of 'a batchelor of artes of Magdalen hall Sir Parkes (who) hanged himself because he was put back and not ordained at Oxon at ye ordination december 23.1632; he was a very civill studious youth'.

66

THE SEVENTEENTH-CENTURY CURATE

Curates continued to starve in the seventeenth as well as in the sixteenth century. In the Kentish petitions that were sent to Parliament in 1643 there were frequent allusions to ill-paid curates. At Ore the stipend was £8 per annum, and so the curate was compelled 'to steal meat for himself and his'; and on being caught red-handed confessed that he would rather do it 'than beg or starve'. At Tenterden, the absentee vicar, Dr. Peake, who was also a prebendary of Canterbury and rector of Acris, drew £200 from the living, but only paid his curate 7s. 8d. per Sunday. At Leeds and Broomfield the curate was allowed £12 6s. 8d. for serving both parishes; and at Hucking £10 'at most', which meant that no one would stay there long, and 'wee had noe settled minister amongst us for the space of thirty years past'. In 1623 the churchwardens of Toot Baldon in Oxfordshire presented their parson, William Allen, 'for not paying our curat his wages for the last yeare beyng at Michaelmas last twelve pounds'; Warborough, 'alloweth their curate for his stipend £xi per an'; and at Towersey he received 'by the yere £x'. Sir Thomas Dawes recorded in his diary during 1643 that he classed his curates with his 'almsfolk' and paid them both alike according to a sliding scale based on the price of corn; while Adam Smith compared their stipend to that of a journeyman. Out of fifty-one curates in Lancashire and Cheshire twenty-three were paid £5 or less; but the average stipend was in the region of £7. Some, of course, did very much better and three of them got respectively £52 10s., £40 and £25. Not all the Kentish curates were ill provided for : John Streating of Ivychurch drew an income of £30; and John Terry at Smarden received £20. There were also a number of perquisites, such as surplice fees, but these were not always forthcoming. At Tenterden Dr. Peake refused to allow his curate to preach at a funeral unless the ten-shilling fee was handed over to himself; and as late as 1709 we find the curate, Philip Keene, at Dorchester presenting, 'John Applegarth one of the executors of Richard Applegarth late of Dorchester dead, for not paying me my accustomed dues for burying in the church-

yard being 1s. Lezing widow for not paying my dues for burying her husband in the churchyard being 1s.; Charles Price, John
Clapham, Edward Saywell, John Clerk, Timothy Smith of Dorchester for not paying their severall accustomed dues in the churchyard being 1s. each.' John Applegarth was cited to appear before
the archdeacon's court, where he was ordered to pay 'the said
1s. . . . and also the expenses which he (the judge) taxes in the
Acts at 6s. 8d. at or before the 13th day of July next'. Applegarth replied : 'That he did cause his father to be buried in the
church of Dorchester. But denys to pay 1s. for the same to the
curate by the reason it is contrary to the custome of the parish
as he is informed'. But a former curate testified that he had been
minister at Dorchester for nineteen years, during which time
he had always received 'the said dues for burying'. Subsequently
Applegarth and his companions were all declared to be contum-
acious and were excommunicated.

Despite the improved status of the parochial clergy it was still
difficult to persuade the gentry to educate their children for the
Church. Richard Bernard complained in the early seventeenth
century, as Eachard was to do after the Restoration, that 'they
wish their children anything, worldly lawyers, fraudulent merchants, killing physicians' rather than 'priests . . . because the
proud and wicked despise you'. None the less a few peers' sons
took holy orders prior to the Civil War, including George Herbert,
and Anthony Grey, the eighth earl of Kent; and a fair sprinkling
of the sons of squires and knights. These gentlemen, however,
rarely became stipendiary curates, but were immediately instituted
to a rich benefice. The clergy themselves, who were now producing off-spring in large numbers, provided an increasing percent-
age of candidates for ordination. It has been estimated, for
example, that between 1600 and 1640 the number of sons from
the parsonages of Oxfordshire and Worcestershire rose from five
to twenty-three. But the bulk of the clergy were drawn from the
lower middle classes, the children of tradesmen, merchants, yeomen or farmers; and the purely labouring population gradually

ceased to produce ordinands. Indeed by the beginning of the Civil War there are scarcely any references in Puritan surveys and and petitions to men of very humble origin. There were, of course, exceptions. One of the charges levelled against Edward Heron, rector of Coston in Leicestershire, during 1646 was that he employed a wheelwright and a tanner as his curates. This he firmly denied. Baxter, too, recalled curates at Eaton Constantine in Shropshire who included 'the excellentest stage-player in all the country' and an attorney's clerk, 'who was a drunkard'. Throughout history the clergy have always been drawn from a wide variety of sources, and the seventeenth century was no exception. To name a few well-known clerics : Richard Baxter himself was the son of a 'freeholder, free from the temptations of poverty and riches'; Ralph Josselin was of yeoman stock; Jeremy Taylor the child of a Cambridge barber; and Richard Rogers from the joiner's shop.

The position of the stipendiary curate in 1641 was still no bed of roses, judging from a pamphlet published that year and entitled *The Curates Conference*, which consists of a conversation between two of them, Master Poorest and Master Needham, in St. Paul's Cathedral. Poorest was asked how he did, and replied :

I will deal plainly with you. I staid in the University of Oxford, till I was forced to leave it for want of subsistence. I stood for three of four several scholarships, and though I was found upon examination sufficient, yet I do seriously protest that at one time I was prevented by half a buck and some good wine, that was sent up to make the fellows merry; and, another time, a great lady's letter prevailed against all ability of parts and endowments whatsoever; a third time, the warden of the college had a poor kinsman, and so he got the major part of the fellows on his side, for fear and flattery, that there were no hopes to swim against so great a stream; and so I was forced to retreat into the country, and there turn first an usher, and at last was made curate, under a great prebend, and a double-beneficed rich man, where I found promises beyond performances; for my salary was inferior by much to his cook, or his coachman, nay, his barber had double my stipend; for I was allowed but eight pounds per annum, and to get my own victuals, cloathes, and books as I could; and when I told him the means were too little, he said that, if I would not, he could have my cure supplied by another, rather for less than what I had; and so I was yoaked to a small pittance, for the space of twelve years.

Master Needham had had a similar experience, as he told his friend, in Lincolnshire, where 'the churchwarden is scarce able to give the minister more than a barley bag-pudding to his Sunday dinner'. So they agreed that rather than be a curate it was better to 'be a cobler and sit and mend old shoes'. Needham went on wistfully to suggest the possibility of a strike among curates. 'I wonder,' he asked, 'how these lip-parsons would do, should there be but once a general consent of all the curates to forbear to preach or read prayers but for one three weeks, or a month only; how they would be forced to ride for it, and yet all in vain; for how can one person supply two places at one time twenty miles distance?' But, alas, this was but a pipe-dream and they must be prepared to put up with life as it was. One of the chief thorns in their flesh was often the parson's wife, who 'takes out of the curate's wages, as, half of every funeral sermon, and out of all burials, churchings, weddings, christenings, etc. she hath half duties, to buy lace, pins, gloves, fans, black bags, satin petti-coats, etc.'; and pays for the maintenance of her coach, 'by sub-tracting his allowance at the quarter day'. Needham, who had bought himself a new gown out of a legacy left him by a parish-ioner, found that his incumbent's wife 'had informed her hus-band, that I waxed proud; and advised him to get another in my place'. Master Poorest also suffered at the hands of the lady parson, who refused to allow his parishioners 'out of their loves' to 'give me anything to mend my salary'.

In general they complained that a curate's life consisted of too much work and too little pay. 'It is a strange world', they declared, in which 'they [their employers] should flourish and flow in wealth for doing nothing, and the poor curates, that do all, can get nothing'. These latter endure the heat and burden of the day, reading all the services and preaching all the sermons, while the parsons strutt about in cassocks of damask and silk stockings, hunt, gamble, drink and 'so passeth the time away'. A London curate of Master Poorest's acquaintance had told him : 'most curates in London lived upon citizens trenchers; and, were it not that they were pitiful and charitable to them there was no possibility of subsistence; and that, of late, it went harder with them than before; for ever since the parsons have so enhanced their revenues, the citizens have mainly withdrawn their purses, so now the curate must live upon his set pittance or else starve'. As a result they were reduced to 'one degree above dining with Duke Humphrey', i.e. starve. The upshot of this conversation was that Master Poorest proposed joining a ship to the East Indies as its chaplain; a decision which his friend heartily applauded : 'Excellent well, oh refuse it not; it is far beyond living a-shore for ten pounds per annum'. He himself intended becoming 'a preacher to a regiment of soldiers . . . for we cannot be lower than now we are'. So they parted, after Master Needham had added regretfully : 'I would have given you, Master Poorest, one pint of wine, but ultra posse non est esse [no one can go beyond his ability] as you know.'

Pity the poor curate! But not all of them were quite so industrious, abstemious, and generally above reproach as Masters Poorest and Needham would have us believe. Their small incomes, hard conditions and low social status, not to mention the probability of a wife and large family to maintain, sometimes led them—since as curates-in-charge they were under little effective supervision by their employers—to try and retrieve their fortunes by such dubious activities as betting and gambling, or to seek to drown their sorrows at the local ale-house. Such practices inevitably lost them the respect of their better-class parishioners and occasionally involved them in an exchange of abuse and even of fisticuffs with the less desirable members of their flock, whose growing anti-clericalism took full advantage of the situation.

At the beginning of the century the puritans had been loud in their condemnation of the semi-literate curate, who was still to be found doing duty in the poorer livings. *In A Viewe of the State of the Clargie within the Countie of Essex*, for example, they listed a number of such wretched clerics in scathing terms: at Braxted Parva there was 'onlie a dumb minister', to whom the parson, Mr. Johnson, himself resident in Sussex, 'alloweth £6–13–4 p. an. and this curate alsoe dwelleth three miles from thence'. The curate of Tottam Parva was likewise 'a dumb minister'. Two others were described as 'a dumb minister' and 'a common gamster and serveth for £5–6–8 per ann and his diet'. But by 1640 they had changed their tune; for a puritan survey of that year disclosed that by now the majority of curates were graduates and most of them were preaching, although not always licensed to do so. In the Canterbury diocese, for instance, there was only one non-preacher, who is described as 'Mr. Keth his poor curate'; there was another in Wiltshire, Mr. Hulett, curate of Netherhampton, who persuaded a neighbouring rector to preach for him once a month; but in the large Lincoln diocese none are mentioned. The worst area was Herefordshire, where there were still some twenty-nine dumb curates. Consequently puritanical criticism was now directed against 'weak', 'seelie' and 'erroneous' preachers, or men who did not preach often enough, rather than those who did not preach at all. For some curates were content to mount their pulpits once a fortnight, once a quarter or even once a year, instead of providing the weekly sermon required by the canons. The puritans, indeed, were demanding two sermons per Sunday, but this was contrary to official policy, since in his metropolitical visitation of 1633–6 Archbishop Laud had sought to discourage Sunday afternoon preaching, for which catechising should be substituted. It is interesting to note in passing that a curate of Maidstone in Kent so took this recommendation to heart that he rebuked 'a painefull neighbouring minister', informing him that he 'did much disgrace the clergie by preaching twice on the Sabbath daies; and that preaching in the afternoone was but prating and babling'. The laity would probably not have agreed with him. In neighbouring

Leeds and Broomfield they complained that they 'had not that preaching amongst us as we could desire'; and at Yalding it was said: 'noe preaching Pastor that hath beene conscionable to performe his office faithfully amongst us for the space of thirtie yeares and upwards'. Undoubtedly there were still curates who preferred to expound the gospels and catechism informally from their stalls, rather than to preach a full-blooded sermon.

However, there were graver offences committed by curates than a failure to preach. Robert Conney, curate of Sydenham in Oxfordshire, was accused by his churchwardens in 1609 of 'lyeing suspesiously of incontinency betwene one mistress Marle and mistress Yorke'. A year earlier Richard Jones, curate of Towersey, was presented 'for not catachizinge the youthe of our towne accordinge to the Canons in that behalf provided . . . wee presente Mr. Richard Jones for his absence diverse tymes from his cure and but for the good care of the fermors of the parsonage wee should have lyne destitute often tymes of ordenarie service in the church. Wee doe present Mr. Richard Jones minister to be both a quarreler, a fighter and a drunkard in publicke places upon a common fame'. On 14 March 1625 Joan Coxe of Benson, also in Oxfordshire, confessed: 'That she hath had a childe unlawfully begotten of which Mr. John Shurlock the Curat of Benson is the father. . . . Mr. Shurlock before and after the childe was begotten promised to marry her but he durst not doe it untill his father was dead.' John Woodcocke, curate of Littlehampton, Sussex, was found to be so much 'in drincke' one day during 1622 that he could not bury a child, 'but Mr. Thimble then minister of Ford did bury it'.

The Kentish petitions of 1641 contain a number of references to unsatisfactory curates: John Terry, curate of Smarden, for example, was accused of many things. 'The said Mr. Terry hath bene negligent in the dutyes of his callinge; so that, when the congregation have been come together one the Lord's day, hee hath bene absent, none knowinge where, or one what occasion: when corpse have bene to be buried, he hath bene soe distem-

pered with beere that he could not read the burial. The said
Mr Terry (being a man much inclined to the horrid vice of
drunkenes) doeth often frequent blind and unlycensed alehouses,
wherein he hath bene soe overtaken in the said vice, that he hath
bene found lyinge in the streete and dirt, not able to help him-
selfe, but two men have lead him to his house.' His rector, Robert
Elye, turned a blind eye on such misdemeanours; and in fact was
himself accused of systematically placing 'curates with us, from
time to time, soe negligent in their callings, and vitious in their
lives and conversacions as are very offensive and greaveous unto
us'. He paid them about £20 per annum. Another Kentish incumbent, Robert Barrell of Maidstone, was also said to have
'many curates under hym, most of them being pott companions,
of a verie scandalous and of a very evill life, one of them leaving
a bastard child behind him in our towne, and others of them
gamsters; many of them coussining and defrauding poore tradesmen, by getting their goods into their hands, and then running
away; few of them but idle, unable, unapt to teach.'

One of the curate's principal tasks was to catechise 'youth and
ignorant persons' of his parish for at least half-an-hour on Sunday
afternoons; and parents, employers and householders were held
responsible for seeing that their children, servants and apprentices
attended such a catechism. None the less it was not always easy
either to persuade them to come, or when they arrived to behave
with reverence and decorum. The churchwardens of Coldwal-
tham in Sussex reported in 1622, 'Hee [the curate] doth catachise,
and some cometh, and some are obstinate and will not . . . there
are some, as we have heard, that doe not carry themselves so
reverently towards our minister as they should doe'. A year later
the lads and lasses of Yapton in the same county were found
dancing on Sunday afternoons to the tune of a fiddler from Boxgrove. 'Many youth in Yapton,' the archdeacon was informed,
'when they should be in church on those Sundays to be catechised,
are then attending on him to dance.'

The Puritans objected to men whom they termed 'dumb and

scandalous ministers'; but the Anglican Church Authorities were equally opposed to fanatical puritan clergymen, who refused to wear the surplice, omitted the use of the ring in marriage and the cross in baptism, failed to conduct their services strictly in accordance with the Prayer Book rubrics, and preached the pure doctrines of Geneva when they should merely have been reading one of the authorised homilies. The curate of Towersey, the notorious Richard Jones, for instance, was presented by his churchwardens 'for not wearinge his surplis uppon the sabot day at Eveninge prayer at the christninge of a childe. And also upon Easterday, and divers other Sabothe dayes'. A more notorious case was that of John Crosse, an ex-grocer's assistant, who became curate of Scammonden chapel in the parish of Huddersfield. He was unlicensed, but was nonetheless encouraged by his vicar, John Smith, to preach both at Scammonden and in Huddersfield parish church, where he attracted great crowds and, according to witnesses, publicly condemned the use of the cross in baptism, the wearing of the surplice and non-preaching ministers. He was prosecuted during 1617–18 on the following charges:

That the said John Crosse hath publiquely and privately taught and defended or mainetained all or the moste of the erroneous opinions following vizt. That all unpreachinge ministers ar dumble doggs, and damned persons and whosoever goeth to heare them cannot be saved; Item that noe preacher sanctifieth the Saboath or is a sanctified person, or lawfully called to the ministry unlesse he preache twice every Saboath; Item that it is not lawfull to dresse meate or doe any such thinge on the Saboath day; Item that the signe of the Crosse in baptisme, wearinge of the surplesse in time of divine service and other laudable rites and ceremonies of this Churche of England are damnable and antichristian; Item that it is not lawfull to use the Lords praier nor any other forms prescribed in the booke [i.e. Prayer Book] . . . affirmeinge noe praier is available but that whereunto the spirit at that time moveth and all other is damnable. . . . That the said John Crosse by suche his phantasticall and irregular proceedings . . . hath gathered after him many followers persons of litle or noe understandinge, discontented in mind and not well affected to our present Churche government,

sundry of whom beinge taughte by the said John Crosse have openly
affirmed that the signe of the Crosse in baptisme is the marke of
the beaste in the Revalation, others by his strange doctrine have
been distracted and driven into madnesse, and forsaike theire ordinary trades and callings to follow him whether he list to goe.

He was condemned, dismissed from his post and ordered to
pay £8 costs. Many other curates also had their licences withdrawn when they refused to conform to the 1604 canons, although
the exact number is not known. But in the Lincoln diocese alone
nine of them lost their jobs. Curates, of course, could be got rid
of much more easily than incumbents, since they did not possess
the protection of the freehold; and no doubt many conformed,
although privately unconvinced, in order to safeguard their precarious position, when dismissal could well mean starvation for
themselves and their families. John Carter, curate of St. Peter
Mancroft, Norwich, told his parishioners in 1636 at the height
of the Laudian persecution : 'There is another part of the divine
service to be read; but I am commanded by authority to read it
in another place, viz. at the communion table : and so commanded
I must do it or leave my ministry. I hope no judicious christian
will be offended at it, seeing it cannot possibly be unlawful to
read the same service in any part of the church being the whole
temple of the House of Prayer . . . the magistrate hath power to
command it; and we are to preach and practice obedience to
governors. Therefore it cannot be accounted a sufficient cause
for any man to leave his ministry. God make us carefull in the
manie things that concern our salvation'. None the less his conscience would not let him rest, and eventually he was suspended
for not reading the second service in the proper place. But when
the congregation paid the piper it was a different story; for then
the curates were often more afraid of their parishioners than the
bishop. William Kerrington and Thomas Warren, who were
curates of St. Lawrence and St. Nicholas, Ipswich, were 'admonished by the Chancellor [Richard Corbett] to observe the Orders
of the Church and to certify their performance at the next Court

after Whitsuntide'. To which Warren replied that they dared not observe the Orders of the Church for fear of losing their income, which came solely from the parish : a typical enough instance of Puritanical parishioners refusing to pay the stipends of those curates whose theological opinions differed from their own. For as the Puritans were forced more and more upon the defensive by Archbishops Bancroft and Laud, they sought to restore the balance by setting up Sunday afternoon lectureships in the towns, which were financed by their well-to-do supporters and filled by curates anxious to increase their stipends as well as to preach the pure Word of God unfettered by the need to wear the surplice or to use the Prayer Book. Furthermore between 1625 and 1633 a group of wealthy London non-conformists clubbed together to purchase impropriated tithes, lands and advowsons, with the avowed object of reforming and purifying the Church of England by installing and supporting as many Calvinistic ministers as possible in livings, lectureships and schools, who would be selected and controlled by themselves. In particular these 'feoffees for impropriations' as they were called favoured 'removable' men, i.e. unbeneficed clergymen, over whom the bishops had little or no power. This type of 'godly' preacher was to be trained through the Calvinistic St. Antholin lectureships in London and then dispersed throughout England to fill the large number of ecclesiastical offices now at the disposal of the feoffees. Their accounts disclose that the following substantial sums were paid to curates during this period : Zachary Symmes, curate of Dunstable, received £20 a year for seven years in addition to the profits of the living; Stephen Geree, curate and lecturer at Wonersh, Surrey, was paid £60 a year for more than five years; Alexander Gregory, curate of Cirencester, got £10 a year for four years and £20 for a fifth, over and above his regular income; and Boras Coxall, curate of South Malling in Sussex, received an augmentation of £10 per annum for three and a half years. This organisation was finally forcibly dissolved in 1633; but the puritanical lectureships continued, although they came under

The Orthodox true Minifter,

the Seducer and falfe Prophet.

Fig. 3.

increasing fire as Laudianism reached its peak in the late 1630s. By 1638 most of the extreme puritanical lecturers had been ousted, and the rest forced to conform. The bishops themselves appointed what were known as 'combination-lecturers', who wore the surplice and hood, read the Prayer Book services, and invariably took the second service at the communion table. The following year the majority of bishops certified to Archbishop Laud 'that everything is well'.

Anglican curates as well as incumbents suffered severely during the Great Rebellion. The following disgraceful scene took place in Radwinter parish church during June 1642 : 'The curate entering the desk to say evening prayer was told by Edward Montford that if he went to prayers he and his companions would go ringing. The curate replied they would answer it to authority. However in the middle of the Confession, Montford, Crowland, Chapman and one Waite a stranger, all animated by Montford who would bear them out, began to jangle. That done, in the Psalm and Lesson Montford especially derided the words which were read, with blasphemous answers, impious mockeries, unseasonable Amens; crying out, 'Hold your peace, Hob; down on your knees, Hob,' with much laughter; scornfully pulling off his hat and clapping it on again; bending the knee and bidding others to do so in derision while the lessons and hymns were reading; then went they again to chime and jangle, with incredible performances as words and gestures, and so out of church. But when they came at the church gate they returned again, with what intent God knows. Montford, Crowland and Waite came immediately up to the reading pew, told the curate they must pray with him, opened the door, came in, thrust him out; whereupon he departed with silence. "Now I like your obedience", quoth Montford; Crowland told him he had been well enough served to have been taken by the heels and had his brains beaten out.' The selfsame curate suffered a further humiliation at a funeral : 'After a burial in the churchyard widow Seaman and the wives of Richard Smith, Henry Smith, Samuel and Henry Reef and

Josias Ward, coming impudently upon the curate as he was passing from the grave, laid violent hands upon him, drew their knives and . . . cut and rent off his surplice and hood in a barbarous manner before the whole congregation; and so carried away their spoils, triumphing in their victory.'

Among the 2,425 loyalist clergy deprived during the Great Rebellion and Interregnum there were a number of curates, some of whom, however, were able to obtain re-employment. Many of them were charged with a long string of so-called offences in order to justify their eviction; but their wives and families were usually entitled to a fifth of their stipend after their ejection. Those debarred from further clerical work often suffered considerable hardship and earned their living as best they could: some by schoolmastering, others by returning to those secular occupations they had quitted when they took holy orders, others again by taking refuge in the homes of charitable friends or relations and awaiting better times; but many died in dire poverty before those times arrived. Not a few actively espoused the royal cause or joined underground resistance movements like the Clubmen, and suffered physical injury and imprisonment in consequence. Some fled abroad and one at least joined the Church of Rome. Here are some of their stories:

Robert Grimer, curate of Wicken, Cambridgeshire, was ejected by the earl of Manchester in 1644 because, or so witnesses deposed, he observed Bishop Wren's injunctions; published the *Book of Sports*; told his parishioners, 'if they would not help him to more meanes [his stipend was £14 8s. per annum] they should perish for want of teaching'; never exhorted people to take the Covenant; 'a great swearer and a sticker'; had a man excommunicated for not paying his tithes, and on his dying left his body unburied for days until his relatives obtained absolution. Subsequently Grimer was imprisoned and debarred from the ministry.

Joseph Chamberlain, curate of Little Maplestead in Essex, was charged with frequenting ale-houses, refusing people the sacrament unless they took it at the altar rails, reading the homilies, since the parish would not pay for his licence to preach, often leaving his church unsupplied, and saying he would read the mass 'if anyone hired him to do so'.

Even more reprehensible was John Brawne, curate of Compton Abdale, Gloucestershire, who had 'never preached in twenty years, often absent months together'; while William Holdsworth, curate of Earl Shilton, Leicestershire, was said to have 'delivered old notes as new sermons for the past 20 years'. Other curates were cited before their County Committees and deprived for such sins as ignoring the Directory, reviling members of Parliament and refusing to pray for them, provisioning royalist soldiers, excommunicating their churchwardens, raising and sending money to Oxford for the king, and refusing the Covenant and Engagement. A good number were accused of moral offences, especially drunkeness, swearing and immorality: Maptid Violet, curate of Aldeburgh in Suffolk, was indicted in 1644 'for drunkeness, singing ribald songs at Inns, at an inn invaded a woman's bedroom at midnight with a jug of beer to get her to drink with him'. One of the town bailiffs wrote of Violet to the earl of Manchester's chaplain, T. Good, 'that base Antinomian is like to be intertayned at Hallisworth and teach them Libertinisme, who need no spurring. I wish you could procure a warrant; it might scare him to his wife in Norfolk.'

Two witnesses deposed before the Wiltshire County Committee on 3 October 1646 that Samuel Maynston, curate of Nunton, 'came back drunk from Sarum, kissed all the maids in church, gave each a "tuttye", and sent them away without catechizing . . . a woman of Downton would affirme that hee offered to be unchast with her'. Richard Carpenter, curate of St. James's, Duke's Place, London, was ejected because 'some fowle things were informed against him', when he went over to the Church of Rome. Another so-called drunkard, John Allen, curate of Capel in Surrey since 1632, was sequestered by the Committee for Plundered Ministers on 8 January 1644–5, being accused among other things of concocting a charm for getting rid of tooth-ache, 'saying that yf the party greeved would believe it would helpe him'; and a curate named Alexander of Uffington, Lincolnshire, actually had the temerity to board at an ale-house and encourage his parishioners to come to him after evening service 'and spend their pence with him'. Oliver Thorowgood, who combined a curacy at Bromham, Bedfordshire, with the vicarage of Mel-bourn, Cambridgeshire—a not uncommon example of a curate who was also an incumbent—lost them both on being convicted as 'the father of a bastard child'.

Some of them were roughly handled. It was said of Edward Lane, curate of West Bromwich, Staffordshire, 'that after many other affronts he was pulled out of the reading desk one Sunday by rebels, who dragged him into the churchyard to see the surplice and prayer book burnt: imprisoned for many years: died in 45th year just before 29 May 1660'. When William Bridges, who was the curate of his relative, Dean Scott, read the common prayers in the church of Barwick-in-Elmet, Yorkshire, he too was attacked by Parliamentary soldiers; and Richard Bourn, curate of Cannock in Staffordshire, was severely wounded by a soldier whilst officiating there in 1648. Some of those who had been deprived, however, managed later to slip back into the Church. Thomas Hill, who was a student of Christ Church, Oxford, and curate of St. Thomas, Sarum, was sequestered by the Wiltshire County Committee in 1643. But shortly afterwards he became first curate and then vicar of Black Bourton, Oxfordshire; and in 1650 rector of Wylye, Wiltshire. None the less he had not changed his spots, since he forbade his curate to read out Parliamentary orders. John Robins, who had been ousted from a curacy at Ramsey, Huntingdonshire, by the Committee for Plundered Ministers in 1647, is found officiating at Bury St. Edmunds in 1650; and John Horsborough, ejected from the curacy of Walls-end, Northumberland, in 1647, was serving Bamburgh in 1650, and was still there nine years later.

The families of curates, like those of incumbents, were usually provided for. When, for instance, Ely Turner, curate of Monken Hadley, Middlesex, was sequestered in September 1644, the Committee for Plundered Ministers granted a fifth of the stipend to his wife, Anne; and after he vacated the cure in 1650, fifths were also paid to his two daughters. Again Richard Avey, curate of Putney, Surrey, since 1632, who was ejected on 5 May 1647, had the satisfaction of knowing that the County Committee had given a fifth of his income to his son, Thomas. Occasionally a curate refused to take his eviction lying down: John Blemel of St. James's, Bury St. Edmunds, Suffolk, was imprisoned for forbidding his parishioners to pay tithes to the intruding minister, S. Crossman; and Timothy Hutton, curate of St. Giles, Cripplegate, was sent to the King's Bench prison for 'locking the church against a newly elected lecturer, J. Sedgwick'.

The most heinous offence, of course, was either to serve in the royal forces or assist an underground movement against Parliament. George Wilson, curate of Fleckney, Leicestershire, was sequestered in 1645 'for being in arms against Parliament'; and John King, curate of St. Thomas, Sarum, was a member of the Wiltshire Clubmen, who openly wore their white ribbon in his hat and 'entertained malignants at his house, where there were great disorders'. He was long imprisoned. On the other hand a curate could be deprived simply for inadequacy: William Hutton of Sadberge, Durham, who tried to appease Parliament by taking the Covenant and promising to preach twice of a Sunday, was none the less 'ejected for insufficiency' in 1651.

Those curates, however, who remained in the Church began to find life easier. The Puritans had long condemned pluralities, and now a serious attempt was made to abolish them, with the avowed object of providing an independent and secure livelihood for as many clergy as possible.

> Bigamy of steeples is a hanging matter,
> Each must have one and curates will grow fatter.

83

Pluralists were usually given the option as to which of their livings they would keep; but if they refused voluntarily to relinquish either of them, then they were deprived of the richer one.

Unfortunately this enlightened measure was coupled with a campaign to discontinue tithing that frightened away many would-be ordinands; although in fact they were never abolished since it was found that the clergy could not be paid adequately without them. And for the same reason pluralities came creeping quietly back again. Furthermore in order to provide a truly living wage in face of rapidly rising prices, the Trustees for Maintenance found themselves obliged to augment stipends out of the proceeds of the sale of royalist estates and episcopal and capitular lands.

The yawning gaps in the ranks of the clergy caused by the disruptions and ejections of the Civil Wars had to be filled, even if that meant lowering clerical standards. Educated laymen, schoolmasters in particular, were therefore encouraged to preach and become readers and lecturers with a view to ultimate ordination. Two striking illustrations of this policy are to be found in the autobiographies of Henry Newcome and Adam Martindale. Henry Newcombe, after leaving the university of Cambridge in 1647, began to teach at Congleton school in Cheshire, when he also acted as reader to Mr. Ley at Astbury and preached in both Congleton and Astbury churches before being ordained on 22 August 1648. He then went as curate to Goosetree, 'where,' he wrote, 'it pleased God I had the unanimous consent of the whole chapelry under their hands and there I preached a year and a half'. In fact he preached there twice every Sunday; and prayed six times every day, twice with his wife, twice in secret, and twice with his family. His wife's kinsman, Henry Manwaring, allowed them to lodge in his own house of Kermingham, and was instrumental in procuring Newcome his first living, the rectory of Gawsworth, some two years later. 'I have oft spread his kindness to me before the Lord,' declared the latter, 'and have prayed he would repay it, that he might some way fare better for his love to me'.

Adam Martindale served a longer apprenticeship. His school-days at St. Helen's in Lancashire had certainly not enamoured him with the Church, since he was taught by 'an humdrum curate, that had almost no scholars, nor deserved any, for he was both a simpleton, and a tipler'. During the Civil War he himself acted as a lay chaplain to the Parliamentary forces in Liverpool, where he enjoyed the 'sweet communion' of the officers of the garrison, and where on its surrender he suffered imprisonment for a while. After his release he became a schoolmaster at Whiteley, engaged on an intensive course of study, and began to preach in neighbouring churches. In 1645 he received a 'call' to Gorton, which he accepted 'upon condition that I might have the uni-versall consent of the chappelrie', which was readily forthcoming. Previously he had refused an assistantship at Middleton worth £13 per annum rather than 'thrust out my poore old master'—the very curate whom he had once so bitterly criticised—'under pretence of supplying his place, and that he being a decrepid man with a charge, and possibly might find it difficult to get another place' : a true act of christian charity and of returning good for evil. None the less at Gorton Martindale found himself faced by many problems. His lack of ordination prevented him from baptising or celebrating Holy Communion, the parishioners failed to make good their promise to pay him an adequate salary, and he found the whole place rent by theological divisions be-tween the Presbyterians and the Independents. In vain he sought to compose their differences. 'I was desirous,' he wrote, 'to meddle of no side, but only to preach the Gospell to them'; but as that proved impossible he added, 'I would faine have removed out of this hot climate into a cooler, but the people would not heare of it, and had me so fast that I could not get away honestly without their consent'. Yet when at last he plucked up the necessary courage to resign, clerical assistants of any kind were so thin on the ground that he was promptly offered five places in Cheshire and another three in Yorkshire. He was much attracted to the latter county, but before he could make a move the vicarage of Rostherne in Cheshire was offered him in 1649, which he accepted in the face of considerable opposition that blocked his acceptance by the Manchester classis, and compelled him to go to London instead for his ordination. The opposition, however, continued and his thirteen years at Rostherne were by no means easy ones. His career illustrates at once both the difficulty of recruiting clergy and the problems they had to contend with in these troubleous times even when they found themselves on the winning side.

The Restoration Settlement saw a great dearth of clergy, which was further increased by the Bartholomew ejections of 1662 that deprived the Church of 1,760 ministers, of whom 220 were lecturers, assistants and curates serving chapels of ease. These last were especially numerous in Lancashire. But the majority of those ejected did not move far from their old parishes, unless compelled to do so by the Five Mile Act of 1666, and under the Declaration of Indulgence in 1672 were often licenced to officiate there or elsewhere in the same county. Their sufferings, if not so great as those of the Anglicans during the Great Rebellion and Interregnum, since they were rarely rabbled, were none the less considerable. Deprived of their livelihood and generally speaking lacking private means, they turned to trade or farming. The learned professions such as law, medicine, teaching or private chaplaincies and tutorships were officially forbidden them, but none the less they engaged in these occupations whenever feasible. 'A country minister,' it was said, 'if he were a man of parts and enterprise, might doctor his neighbours' ailments, school some of his children and keep a small farm into the bargain, provided the local justices were not hostile.' A great deal of course depended upon how strictly the law was enforced. A large number persisted in their preaching and were either paid by their congregations or received charitable relief from wealthy benefactors. The married ones with large families were especially hard hit. Richard Baxter wrote of one of these Bartholomew martyrs: 'I have heard but lately, of a good man, that was fain to spin as women do, to get something towards his family's relief . . . and being melancholy and diseased, it was but part of the day that he was able to do that'. Their prosecution under the law was intermittent: 215 were imprisoned for preaching under the Five Mile Act; there was another outburst of persecution after the Rye House Plot; and in 1685 the non-conformist clergy were incarcerated whole-sale because of the alarm caused by the Monmouth Rebellion. Eight ministers actually died in prison. Fines were freely imposed on those caught preaching; but on the other hand in certain parts of the country they were able to preach for years without being disturbed. Calamy records the names of some thirty non-conformist clergy who continued to occupy their churches or chapels of ease without molestation.

Here are the stories of a few of these non-conforming curates. It was said of John Allen, curate of Yarmouth: 'After his being silenced, he took a house at Goulstone [Gorleston, Suffolk], which is a place out of the jurisdiction of the bishop of Norwich, and often preached there'. John Angier of Denton near Manchester retained his curacy until 1677, but without conforming. 'Warrants were now and then issued to apprehend him, but the worst of Men had no heart to meddle with him. Sometimes they searched, but professed they would not see him for a hundred pounds. Some of the Bishops of Chester would enquire of his son, "how doth the good old man, Mr. Angier?".' James Birdwood, after being evicted from the curacy of St. Petrock near Dartmouth, kept a school there and preached at Batson in the parish of Malborough, but quickly got into trouble. 'One Beer or Bear . . . together with another justice, the Parson of the Parish, a very busy man; and a crew of informers, who were at the beck of the parson and justices were let loose upon him.' He was heavily fined and become so poor that he had to depend upon the charity of his friends. Another impecunious curate was James Bradshaw of Hindley near Wigan in Lancashire, who was constantly in and out of prison. We are told that he 'preached frequently where others of his brethren durst not . . . he had a numerous family of children and was in but strait circumstances, but he bore up with great cheerfulness'.

A number of ex-curates received help and protection from private patrons: Thomas Brook of Congleton in Cheshire was permitted by Sir William Moreton to use his private chapel at Old Moreton Hall for preaching in after his ejection; Hugh Everard, when he was turned out of his curacy at Hickleton, Yorkshire, was taken into Sir John Jackson's household, where he became chaplain and his wife the housekeeper; and Joseph Moore, curate of Sandacre, Derbyshire, 'after his ejectment spent the rest of his time in divers private families, in praying and preaching and catechising'. Richard Clantrye, curate of Weeford in Staffordshire, combined his preaching with farming: 'For he would go in the twilight, to escape the informers, with a Bible in his pocket and a fork on his shoulder . . . he preached as long as he could stand, and longer too; being at last drawn in a chair, out of the parlour into a larger room, for the greater convenience of the Assembly.' Some of them were physically assaulted. John Cooper, who was curate of Cheltenham at the Restoration, suffered 'abuses from intemperate and riotous men, which broke his health and hastened his end'; Edward Lemington, curate of Lemington, Gloucestershire, was also attacked soon after the king's return while entering his pulpit and was forcibly ejected from the parsonage by the old returning incumbent; and John Haddesley, curate of Rockbourne in Hampshire, who had originally been deprived in 1662, but permitted to officiate under the 1672 Declaration of Indulgence, as soon as that indulgence was withdrawn was 'seized in his own house and committed by the Mayor and Recorder of the City to the Common prison'.

Others fled abroad: Matthew Hill of Thirk in Yorkshire settled in Maryland, because, as he told Richard Baxter, when he was in England 'my bookes were too few to buy mee bread'. But Richard

Hincks, curate of Tipton near Wolverhampton, who had helped
Lambert against Monk, was treated very generously by his successor. 'He had,' we are told, 'a wife and many children; but God
provided for him. His successor, Mr. John Taylor, suffered him
to dwell in the parsonage house upon easy terms, tho' he preached
there in the time of public worship'. George Long of Newcastle-
under-Lyme also escaped abroad with his seven children to Ire-
land; Humphrey Philips, assistant at Sherborne in Dorset, who
became chaplain and tutor in the household of John Bampfield
of Poltimore, Devon, later fled to Holland; and Francis Tallents,
curate of St. Mary, Shrewsbury, travelled on the continent with
pupils after his eviction, when it was alleged he had turned
Jesuit.

Some curates, on the contrary, conformed rather than face
the continued rigours of exile. Edward Hollingshead, who had
been deprived of the curacy of Ashford in Derbyshire, accepted
instead that of Fairfield in 1668; Robert Jago, assistant at Wen-
dron, who at first had been a most zealous non-conformist, being
put into jail for defaming the liturgy, suddenly changed his opinions: 'As soon as he came out of prison,' wrote Edmund Calamy,
'a benefice being offered him, he conformed and afterwards lived
but scandalously'; and Timothy Root, curate of Sowerby Bridge
near Halifax, became curate of Howden in 1685. His old friends
'thought his complying after such sufferings so extraordinary that
they wanted to know whether he saw with clearer eyes than they
and desired he would give them an account of the reasons of his
proceeding. But he declined to give them any satisfaction.' Another curate who conformed, Thomas Spatchet of Leeds in Kent,
was licensed to Cookley in 1672, but was believed to have done
so under the influence of a woman's witchcraft and suffered in
consequence from fits for many years. At the opposite end of the
scale Jeremiah Marsden, the former curate of East Ardsley, Yorkshire, who refused to take the oath of allegiance and was declared
to be a rigorous separatist, was fined and imprisoned many times
for sedition, eventually dying in Newgate prison in 1683–4. The

king wrote to the Duke of Buckingham on 7 July 1662 that 'factious' meetings were being held in Leeds and Wakefield organised by Marsden, and ordered his arrest. Later he was involved in the Farnley Wood Plot when he was described as 'a chief contriver of the conspiracy and a trusted agent of the separatist congregations'. Yet another cruelly-used curate was John Mott of King's Bromley, Staffordshire, who was not only driven out of his parish but compelled to abandon his wife, and dared not even attend the funeral of his child or stay 'to comfort his wife under her motherly grief'.

Financially some of them were in desperate need. Samuel Taylor, curate of Edstaston near Wem in Shropshire, who had a wife and nine children, became heavily in debt; James Walton, curate of Shaw near Prestwick in Lancashire, was declared to be 'provided with no substance when ejected, tho' he had several children'; and Thomas Wilson, curate of Lamesley in County Durham, was 'wanting supply . . . very poor, he has nothing from his people, disabled from preaching by the stone'.

During the Interregnum there had been a sharp decline in the number of graduates taking holy orders. This was now rectified. Between fifty-seven and sixty-three per cent of all the men ordained into the Exeter diocese between the years 1660 and 1663 were graduates; while at Oxford Bishop Skinner admitted thirty-one graduates out of a total of thirty-seven candidates for holy orders on 20 September 1663. Nathaniel Lord Crewe, bishop of Durham, who ordained 373 men between 1674 and 1721, estimated that at least 212 held university degrees. But in order to secure sufficient numbers the rules in other ways were somewhat relaxed : ordinations were frequently held *extra tempora*, i.e. out of the ordinary times; and many men were ordained deacon and priest on the same day. Neither was it always possible for the bishops to pick and choose. Peter Mews, bishop of Bath and Wells, informed Archbishop Sheldon in 1675 : 'It is my very great unhappiness to be infested with some so grossly ignorant that they are not able to perform their duties with any tolerable reputation to the Church; and more such are daily creeping in and will certainly be the ruin of it, if not timely prevented.'

Curates in particular were in short supply; and pluralists unable to obtain one got over the difficulty by persuading neighbouring incumbents to fill the gap and thus supplement their own incomes. Here are some examples from the archdeaconry of Nottingham during the latter half of the century: Francis Thorpe, rector of Treswell and vicar of South Leverton employed Thomas Godfrey, vicar of Broughton, to serve his other cure of Cotham Chapel; Michael Richards, vicar of Colston Bassett, served the parish of Holme Pierrepont for many years as the assistant of old John Rustat, rector of Widmerpool; Edward Wilson, vicar of Elkesley, did duty at Gamston for the rector of Pleasley; John Fox, vicar of Basford, ministered at Radford for its non-resident incumbent, John Vickars; and Leonard Curtays, vicar of Wilford, in 1676 was acting as assistant curate in the two parishes of St. Anne and St. Michael, Sutton Bonnington, which were seven or eight miles distant from his own benefice. Sometimes this became a standing arrangement that persisted through a number of incumbencies, as for instance between Orston, with its chapelries of Thoroton and Scarrington, and Whatton-cum-Aslockton.

There were, however, still plenty of pluralists in the same archdeaconry who were employing genuine full-time curates: Francis Clarke engaged Michael Smithurst to do duty in three of his five rural parishes, namely Stoke, Syerston and Elton Chapel; William Wintringham, vicar of East and West Retford paid a curate, John Favell, to serve the latter cure; Robert Field, rector of Hawksworth, had an assistant to minister to his other living of Barton; William Holbrook, rector of Hawton, kept an assistant in his other living of Flawborough; and so the list could be extended *ad nauseam*. But it wasn't only pluralists who kept curates. There were aged or sick incumbents, like Robert Lewis, rector of Stanford, from 1671 onwards for twenty years; and affluent rectors, such as Dr. John Featley of Languar or Dr. John

Lake of Carlton in Lindrick, who employed curates while they themselves retired into semi-seclusion in order to prosecute their studies or their pleasures. Indeed we find curates even in the tiniest of rural benefices. Joseph Quip, the impropriator and curate of Littleborough, was in 1663 keeping an assistant to serve that thinly populated and poor donative. Nicholas Brown, incumbent of the tiny hamlet of West Burton, which could not even provide two churchwardens, employed another; as did also the rectors of the small parishes of Broughton Sulney and Cotgreave. For one reason or another then most livings in the archdeaconry kept curates, whether full-time assistants or part-time incumbents; and this state of affairs is reflected generally throughout the country. But one thing is now clear : it was no longer considered an offence for a curate to serve more than one parish or more than one employer; and this practice quickly became widespread, partly because curates were in short supply, but great demand, and partly because it was a certain and secure, if laborious, means of doubling or trebling one's income. The Reverend Ezekiel Parry, for example, who acted as assistant curate to Robert Thirlby, rector of Clifton, then (1675) at the point of death, was at the same time assisting Thomas Houghton, rector of West Bridgford; and in 1684 John Melson, who served Worksop, was also doing duty at Bothamsall, which was some miles away. Certainly the extra money was needed since the average wage, despite the greatly increased cost of living, was still under £20; and incumbents often drove a hard bargain, especially when their parishes were small, thinly populated and very poor. In April 1684 the churchwardens of St. Anne, Sutton Bonnington, presented their rector, 'for not allowing a sufficient maintenance to Mr. Jo Wild curate'. They further complained that 'we have no prayers but once a fortnight nor upon holy days nor fast days'. A case obviously where no pay produced no work. In such circumstances the curate had often to resort to desperate, and sometimes illegal, expedients in order to make both ends meet. At Aylesbury in Buckinghamshire a neighbouring curate, Francis

Treble, was accused on 8 July 1661 of marrying clandestinely 'in the parish church of Cherley', Manasses Haynes and Alicia Summer, 'without bannes or licence'. He certainly needed the money, judging from his complaints about the way he had been treated by the impropriator's bailiff, John Winter, who was supposed to pay him '£16 and a marke a yeare'; but in actuality 'he foreswore me all and never had I but 20 nobles per annum', which was the original endowment of the parish by Queen Elizabeth, while the rest was supposed to be paid by the impropriator. Winter had also rented out the rectory to his son; 'and yet,' declared Treble, 'I can get nothing at all added to my maintenance.' Furthermore he had cut down trees in the churchyard and annexed monies that had specifically been left to supply bread and wine for the communion. 'Soe,' the curate continued, 'we have nothing now left; for I once bide a communion and when I came to the table there was neither bread nor wine.' He concluded his visitation return to the bishop as follows: 'By me Francis Treble, curate de Cherdsley, now these 32 years in great affliction, misery and trouble ever since clubbes was turned up trump and so is clubbes still. . . . Alsoe for conformity of coming and keeping the church and divine service we all three (curate and two churchwardens) attest and affirm, that there is not one man nor woman in the parish of Cherdsley but keeps the church and divine service duely. I dare compare with any parish in Buckinghamshire. I never had but two and by my conference and frequenting of them I wone them. I wish all the parishes were the like.' He might well ask; for in neighbouring Broughton the churchwardens, William Howe and Anthony Goodridge, presented their curate 'as scandalous for drunckeness and making lewde attempts upon women'.

Treble, however, was by no means the only curate to suffer persecution; but whereas his had been at the hands of the impropriator and his bailiff, Gabriel d'Emilliane, assistant curate at St. Margaret's, Westminster, towards the end of the century, a French Protestant refugee, who had taken Anglican orders, was

most cruelly used by his employer, Dr. Nicholas Onely, prebendary of Westminster Abbey and 'curate-in-charge' of St. Margaret's. Gabriel's case, as he later presented it to his friend, Bishop
Lloyd of Worcester, who was then Lord High Almoner, is so
heart-rending as to warrant quotation in full. He subsequently
in 1701 migrated to America with the help of Dr. Bray, the bishop
of London's commissary for Maryland, who procured him a
special grant of £133 12s. 10d. 'for his own subsistence and to
purchase two Negroes to stock his glebe, he having a family'. He
served Port Tobacco Parish, Charles County, Maryland, for two
years before becoming incumbent of Christ Church, Calvert
County, where he died in 1714.

The case between the Rector Dr. Onely and Gabriel d'Emilliane
his curate in St. Margaret's Parish Westminster.
   When Dr. Onely desired me about four years and a half ago to
come to be his curate, his agreement with me was that he should
allow me £40 a year, but yet so, that he should pay but 7 pounds
quarterly in money, and give me my lodgings for payment of the
rest in the Vicarage house which he enjoys gratis from the parish.
To which I consented, hoping that some perquisites which are
seldom wanting to such places would be a further help to my subsistence, there being no kind of compact or agreement between
us to the contrary. But I was very much surprised when a matter of
ten months after, the Dr. sent for me, and told me, he had two
things to say, which if I would not mend, I could not hold my place
any longer. The first, that I ought not say that he allowed me but
£28 in money yearly and my lodgings, but simply that he gave
me 40 pounds, for the former expression did cast a reflection upon
him. The second thing was that he understood that I took now and
then for myself some money offered to me by way of gifts, whereas
he ought to have all that money himself. I answered him that this
new proposal seemed to me very strange seeing that these things
were distinctly given to me without prejudice to his fees and besides
were very inconsiderable and happened very seldom. And that my
indigent circumstances did not permit me to admit of this new
compact. Whereupon the Doctor grew very hot and gave me very foul
language, and said that he must then turn me out of the place, for
he had sufficiently expressed himself before, that all the money that

was given was to be his. I did not deny indeed but he might have said such words as these, but I thought that in good reason the sense could not be but this, that all the money which was given for him or to him ought to be his, but ought not to extend to a poor gift offered distinctly to his curate without prejudice to his fees. However, seeing him so entirely resolute upon the matter, I told him that rather than go out of the place, when anything of that kind was given, I would bring it faithfully and lay it down before him, and then if his conscience would let him, he might take possession, though I would never part by a new compact with the propriety of it. So being very angry he said he did not care which way he had it, if I did but bring it to him. Which thing I continued for sometime to do, and the Dr. seemed well appeased putting all these small things given to me into his own pocket. Till some months after, growing something more uneasy at this extortion of his, I had a mind to try again whether the Dr. could not be brought to a handsomer dealing. The opportunity which I took was this:

A Gentlewoman in Charles Street having her child christened gave the Clerk the money both for his fees and the Doctor's and then coming to me gave me a crown-piece and told me before the company that she was told with a great deal of amazement to herself that the Doctor very unjustly did extort anything of a gift that was made to his Curates, and therefore she would be well understood as to the giving of this crown, for she did not intend it nor any the least part of it to the Doctor but only to me, as knowing, said she, that I was a very laborious man, and had a poor family to support, whereas the Doctor was too rich for her to give him anything besides his due. And if it should happen that he should take it from me, she desired it to be returned, for she would not part with the propriety of it but to the person that she gave it to.

With this I went to the Doctor and acquainted him with the circumstances of the gift. But he flew with such fury and rage against me, and abused me most shamefully calling me rascal and all the ugly names, pushed me by the shoulders out of his study and told me now he had done forever with me, put the money in his own pocket, and since that time, which is about three years and a half ago, he hath been the most unkind man to me that can be imagined, never would speak to me but frowning and in anger, hath invited for all these three years at a great Christmas dinner all the Parish Officers but me, and with an inveterate malice hath watched for any pretence to turn me out; but he had never one given him till now that he thinks he hath found very sufficient ones which he is resolved not to let pass, and they are the following. When I went on the 5th of this instant to carry him his money, he begun thus with me :

Now I am satisfied that you have renounced the Parish for you leave your business to be done by another.

Secondly, you have again renounced the Parish by refusing to do your office in having denied to sign a paper sent to you by the churchwarden which was an affront done to him.

Thirdly, about three weeks ago you made stay a whole day the burying of a child in the churchyard and they were obliged to make use of another minister, you not being in the way.

Fourthly, you had once four shillings sent you to register a child, and you kept the money and never brought it to the Registrar.

Fifthly, at the christening of a child you had an angel given you, and you let me have but 5 shillings of it.

Therefore I turn you out of your place and see to provide yourself against Our Lady Day next.

I was not surprised at this unworthy dealing of the Doctor for it is nothing but what I expected from such a man some time or other. However I answered in order his five articles.

To the first : That the minister whom I had employed to read prayers four or five times for me, was an honest English clergyman newly come into orders, who desired the favour to do it for exercise, and was well liked by the parishioners, and even with the previous consent of the Doctor himself. To which I might have added by way of retorsion that the Doctor must needs have renounced the parish very often, he who hardly preaches once a month, being glad to employ others to do it for him.

To the second : That I had indeed refused to sign a paper because there was a mere lie contained in it which I could not assert. And because I was unwilling too that a very poor man should thereby have a penalty of 5 pounds laid upon him by the craftiness of the churchwarden.

To the third : I answered that I had no kind of notice of that child to be buried, they having brought it to the churchyard at an unusual hour. Viz. at two o'clock in the afternoon while I was gone to dinner into the City, and that I was in the way before the usual time of parish business.

To the Fourth : That he the Doctor knew very well already that

I had made it appear before the Commissioners for the Act for registering christenings and burials, that it was done by a mistake, and why should he be so uncharitable as to think it to have been a wilful error.

To the Fifth and last : I acknowledged that it was even so and that the crown which I kept was a special gift which I was now no more in a condition to part with, especially since my wife being a sickly woman had been obliged for her health to leave off a little school of girls which she kept at home, and which brought in a little money to help housekeeping. That it was not possible for me and my family to live with the small allowance he gave me to look after so large a parish. And could not do otherwise for the future but take for myself those small gifts which have been hitherto the matter of our disputes.

I leave now any reasonable and impartial good man to judge whether Dr. Onely be in the right to turn me out of my place after several years of a laborious service upon such slender accounts. And if he should say further that several of this parish have often complained of me to him, I answer that I do wonder only that they do not make more complaints but especially against himself for keeping but one Curate upon duty in so large a parish. When there is four or five christenings and as many buryings in one day. Sometimes all appointed at the same hour, let anyone judge whether I being alone can possibly satisfy them all at once. And if they have reason to complain for not being served at their time, whether it should not be rather of the Doctor than of myself.

I shall add to this that Dr. Onely hath been not only a hard taskmaster to me but a very unkind landlord, for not considering his small allowance of 28 pounds in money he hath made me pay all the charges and taxes of the house which amount to above 30 shillings yearly. And as if he had undertaken to weary me out of the place he told me not very long ago that now he had repaired the house, but expected for the future that I should do it myself. And accordingly he would not send to mend a great part of the windows which were accidentally beaten down some months ago by the fall of a great tree, and so hath left us exposed to the bitter season of this cold winter. The house is very old and rotten and so if I must be at the charges of repairing 'tis hardly four pounds more a year that can do it. And with what conscience and christianity can he turn me out of my place, he knows that I have a family of five persons and that I am so poor I am not able even now, should I be left to the world, to find them for one month in victuals besides the affront which I do not deserve. For had I been a wicked and debauched man he could not have dealt worse by me.

Therefore I humbly desire this my case may be considered.

Gabriel d'Emilliane*

It is a sad story, but one has to remember that it is a one-sided story and it would be interesting to learn what Dr. Onely, apparently so mean and inhumane, had to say in his own defence. Certainly John Hepworth, instituted to the vicarage of Harewood, Yorkshire, in 1699 had numerous complaints to make about the curate he there found in possession, William Cheldrey. He wrote to Archbishop Sharp of York on 2 September 1699:

I came to the vicarage house about the middle of May last. Mr. Cheldrey desired to have a chamber (called the chapel chamber) which I granted as soon as it was desired. Without his mentioning any more I told him he should have the next chamber to it for a lodging room, both which he doth enjoy; this I did to engage him to be civil, and that we might live peaceably and quietly. Besides all this I have suffered him to officiate as he used to do before I came hither. I permitted him to consecrate the bread and wine when we have the Sacrament of the Lord's Supper, he distributes the consecrated bread and I follow with the cup, as if he was the priest and I the deacon; yet neither this nor any other courteous carriage of mine can oblige him, but he rails against me, calls me (when amongst his companions) hypocrite, and endeavours to alienate the affections of the people from me. . . . I must be at great cost and charge to be titular vicar and Mr. Cheldrey's underling, and to keep him in his place who is altogether unconcerned about it.

Furthermore Cheldrey had become engaged to Hepworth's daughter, without her father's consent, since she had some money of her own and he was 'a sure spend-thrift . . . and has spared no more than £5 in 17 or 18 years' space. . . . Mr. Cheldrey tells her that at my decease he shall enjoy all'. In another letter to the archbishop dated 26 February 1701, Hepworth complained:

* The manuscript (Lloyd-Baker-Sharp mss. Box 4. Bundle W.57) is undated.

98

I am looked upon as a nominal titular vicar only, and so viewed by Mr. Cheldrey. Tho' I'm obliged to read Prayers but once a month, yet he says when Mr. Boulter (the patron) comes down, I must read Prayers every Lord's Day in the morning unless I allow him £10 per annum out of my salary. . . . The congregation can witness with what difficulty I get into the pulpit, being lame and weak in all my lower parts. Mr. Cheldrey tells me that he is Mr. Boulter's curate and not mine and that this living is a curacy not a vicarage. . . . I cannot prevail with our curate to catechise and I cannot do it for reason of my deafness which would expose me to take false answers instead of true. If this insolency be not curbed there will be no living for me here. He endeavours to alienate the peoples' affections from me, and he . . . with my undutiful and indeed unnatural daughter have got Mr. Archer and most of the town on their side. Alas! I would feign live in peace.

John Hepworth vacated Harewood in 1704 and was followed immediately by William Cheldrey, the nominee of the archbishop to whom the living had lapsed after the patron, John Boulter, had refused to consider him a suitable vicar. Boulter wrote to the archbishop on 29 January 1704–5 :

For my absolutely refusing to present Mr. Cheldrey to the vicarage is not the effect of violent hatred. But of an honest desire to perfect and fulfill the designs of my generous predecessors who always thought him a very mean preacher, and a very odd kind of pattern for a great parish of mostly sensible people to imitate.

Not that Boulter was vindictive : 'It ever was my desire of your Grace and ever shall be that he may not be turned out to the wide world', but found 'some other competency'. Should, however, the archbishop persist in making him vicar then the patron washed his hands of him. He would not augment the stipend as he had promised to do, and 'I can but get a lecturer as before. For I assure your Grace I am quite tired with riding several miles when I am in health to hear a sermon at any of the neighbouring churches'. Cheldrey held the living of Harewood from 1705 to 1724.

Archbishop Sharp certainly had a soft spot in his heart for

curates. While rector of St. Giles-in-the-Fields from 1675–6 to 1691 he treated his own most generously; judging from the following passage in his son's biography of him :

He gave it in charge to his curates in their course of visiting the sick, never to take gratuities from ordinary tradesmen, or any of the inferior sort of people; and that they might be the less tempted to complain of this injunction, he not only sett off to them for their allowance, such fees of his parish (as raised their stipend in some years to six score pounds each) but he declined as much as he could, the performing, in his own person, all those offices where extraordinary perquisites were to be of course expected, that his curates might receive the benefit of his people's generosity.

Curates had their virtues as well as their misfortunes and backslidings; so we may well conclude this chapter with the following tribute paid by the churchwardens of Selsey to their minister when making their returns at the archdeacon's visitation in the year 1662–3. The curate in question was deputising for Dr. Philip King and was 'sent hither by speciall mandate from the Lord Bishopp of Chichester'. The churchwardens continued :

He is constantly resident amongst us, and hath not hitherto been absent; our curate doth use the whole forme and words prescribed in the Booke of Common Prayer; for the tyme he hath been with us, he hath bidden and observed such holy dayes as have fallen out; hee hath preached hitherto twice everie Sonday; he doth purpose to enstruct and catechise the youth, the dayes being longer and the weather warmer; hee is an orthodox divine, preaching sound doctrine, and is farre from sedicious and schismaticall doctrine; our minister doeth not appoint any publique or private fasts, etc., more than what is commanded by authoritye and appointed in the Booke of Common Prayer; our minister is a man of grave and sober life and conversation, and is unblameable in his life and doctrine; his apparell grave and decent as becometh his profession.

CHAPTER V

The Eighteenth-Century Curate

The position of the assistant curate had improved very little if at all by the beginning of the eighteenth century. The universities were now turning out would-be ordinands in large numbers, but many of them experienced difficulty in finding employment. Canon 33 forbade any man to be ordained who had not first secured a title to a curacy, was not already a fellow of his college or an M.A. of five years standing with sufficient private means to support himself at the university. Despite well-known exceptions, however, most of the bishops were not only perfunctory in their examination of candidates, but were equally obliging in turning a blind eye to the fact that many of the titles were purely nominal, supplied by friendly incumbents, who had no real intention of ever employing these curates or paying them a salary. Once ordained they had to fend for themselves and take whatever they could get. Some of them became schoolmasters at a starvation wage and others began by serving as chaplains in the homes of the gentry, where they were often treated very badly, being ordered not only to tutor the children, but to act as grooms or superior servants on a stipend of not more than £10 a year.

Richard Steele recounted how he was expected to retire from his master's table before the sweet was served; and when he declined to do so was promptly given the sack. 'I am a Chaplain,' he wrote, 'to an honourable family, very regular at the hours of devotion, and I hope of an unblameable life; but for not offering to rise at the second course, I found my patron and his lady very sullen and out of humour; though, at first I did not know the reason of it. At length when I happened to help myself to a jelly, the lady of the house, otherwise a devout woman, told me : "It did not become a man of my cloth to delight in such frivolous food". But as I continued to sit out the last course, I was yesterday informed by the butler that "his lordship had no further occasion for my service".'

But for most chaplains discretion was the better part of valour; and he usually retired obediently from the dining-room as desired, 'picking his teeth and sighing with his hat under his arm, whilst the knight and my lady eat up the tarts and the chickens'.

It was the parishes, however, where the growing number of pluralist and non-resident incumbents were looking for cheap curates, that absorbed the majority of the newly ordained. During Queen Anne's reign a Curates' Act was passed in 1713, 12 Anne. 2. c. 12, to secure the 'Better Maintenance of Curates within the Church of England', which contained the following provisions : 'The absence of the beneficed ministers should be supplied by curates that are sufficient and licensed preachers; that these curates should not be employed without the examination and admission of the Bishop of the Diocese . . . that every minister should nominate and present before-hand the person he designs for his curate to the Bishop to be thus admitted and then licensed; that upon granting such licence and admission a sufficient certain stipend and allowance should be appointed by the Bishop under his own hand and seal, to the curate for his maintenance; and in the case of any difference between the minister and his curate, that the Bishop should arbitrate upon the point and cause the settled stipend to be paid.' The sum actually mentioned was 'a sufficient certain stipend or allowance not exceeding £50 and not less than £20 per annum'. This Act was probably more honoured in the breach than the observance; for under the conditions then existing between an incumbent and his assistant it would have been a bold not to say a foolish curate who dared complain to his bishop and invoke its provisions.

At that time there were four categories of curate. First, the stipendiary curates who were employed by non-resident incumbents, and whose stipends, despite the 1713 statute, rarely rose above £20 per annum; secondly, the temporary curates, who were employed to look after sequestered livings or those benefices where the incumbent was sick, otherwise incapacitated, or perhaps even in prison; and thirdly, the assistant curates, who worked either under a resident incumbent or sometimes acted as the colleagues of a stipendiary curate. Finally there was the perpetual curate who served a parish from which the impropriator took all the income, but was legally bound to provide an adequate salary for a priest to undertake the duties. The impropriator was further obliged to nominate him to the bishop for a licence to serve the cure; and when so licensed he became 'perpetual', i.e. he could not be removed at the caprice of the impropriator, only by the bishop. For all practical purposes he ranked as a vicar; and under the provisions of the Pluralities Act of 1838 such perpetual curacies were made into full benefices. 'A Perpetual curate,' it declared, 'has an interest for life in his curacy in the same manner and as fully as a rector or vicar.' However in the eighteenth century the amount of the 'pension' or small money payment allocated to him by the impropriator was usually a very small one. 'The perpetual curate's lot,' wrote G. F. A. Best, 'was the more unhappy in that, certainly lacking tithe-rights and probably lacking glebe, he could never hope to increase his income by the common means of "improvement".'*

Visitation returns, notably those made to Bishops Wake and Gibson of Lincoln between 1706 and 1721, Bishop Secker of Oxford in 1738, and Archbishop Herring of York in 1743, help to make clear the curate's true position. In all too many cases they were supplementing their incomes by serving two or more cures at the same time or by school-mastering; where possible they resided in the parsonage, but sometimes lived in the homes of their patrons, rented a cottage or a couple of rooms, and even put up at the village inn; and their stipends varied enormously from a few pounds to £50 or more per annum. The episcopal

* *Temporal Pillars*, p. 17.

articles of enquiry almost invariably contained one concerning the curate. 'Have you,' it asked the incumbent, 'a licensed curate residing in the parish? or at what distance from it? and who is he? and doth he serve any other and what cure? and what salary do you allow him?' Here are some of the answers.

Lincolnshire. John Jones, who was curate of Aswarby in 1716 drew a salary of '£30 and more'. He also served Demelby, where in 1721 he was 'admonished to perform duty here twice a day'. Mr. Lucas, the curate of Birchfield about the same date, resided at Corby two miles away. Here he was an assistant schoolmaster and lived in the rectory. Robert Holywell, curate of Brocklesby, was only paid £15 and resided a mile from the parish. Miles Hodgson, who was in charge of the sequestrated vicarage of Chalkwell in 1706, received a salary of between £20 and £30, but he was expected to serve Scramblesby as well. He actually lived at Louth where he was also a schoolmaster. The vicar of Corby, as we have already seen, boarded his curate, Richard Lucas, and gave him £20, besides the perquisites of the school. On the other hand the rector of Ferriby only allowed his assist-ant £10; and at Gazton-on-the-Wold the curate received no more than £9. But he lived at Willingham three miles distant, where no doubt he added to his income. Contrariwise the curate of Gedney Hill earned £40; and at Somerby-with-Homeby, which was served by the incumbent's son, he was awarded 'the whole of the benefice'; while at Willingham-by-Stow Thomas Storer drew an income of £30, but resided 'in his own house at Gate Burton rather more than a mile distant'. The curate of Flixburgh, who also served another 'larger cure with the bishop's leave', received a gross income of £65 per annum. These men were the exception rather than the rule and must be set alongside their less fortunate brethren, many of whom got no more than £15, £13 or even £12. Incumbents and curates were not always what they should be. The rector of Burton-by-Lincoln was for some thirty years *sui non-compos* and his duties were performed by a curate living in the household of Sir Henry Monson. William

Green, a deacon, who was in charge of Irby, was declared to be *'ebriosus amovendus'* and his place was taken by the curate of Orby, who received 5s. every other Sunday from the parish.

Oxfordshire. These returns reveal that many curates, despite Canon Law, were still unlicensed. From Waterstock the rector reported: 'I have a curate not licensed, who resides at Queen's College, Oxford, at six miles distance from this place, his name is William Wood A.M. He doth not serve any other cure. His salary I reckon to be about five and twenty pounds a year.' But the curate of Bix, who also served no other church, was paid £40. Thomas Bonnell of Brize Norton took two services and catechised there every Sunday, yet found time to officiate at Yelford every other Sunday: 'He is allow'd £20 per ann and the house, garden and orchard for serving Norton. And £9 pr ann for serving Yelford.' Many of these curates came from Oxford colleges: It was stated, for instance, that at Cassington, 'neither vicar nor curate reside in the parish; but both reside upon their chaplainships at Christ Church in Oxford'; while the vicar of Kidlington declared, 'my curate [James Cosserat] is not licens'd nor doth he reside in this parish, but in Exeter College. This hath been the usual method of supplying ye parish and I never found that ye parishioners ever complained of their being ill served . . . he serves no other cure and the salary he hath is twenty pounds p. ann besides surplice fees and provision for himself and horse with a bed upon occasion whenever he goes thither'. At Newnham Courtney the cure was served, in the rector's absence, by a Mr. Bradley, Fellow of Corpus Christi; and at Sherborne, when the vicar, Thomas Hunt, waited upon 'Lord Macclesfield's family in London, which may be about 18 or 20 weeks in the year', Thomas Bisse, Fellow of All Souls, performed the duty at a charge of 10s. per Sunday. Indeed, as these returns make crystal clear, the average curate's stipend was still in the region of £20 or £30 when serving a single cure, together with surplice fees, other perquisites, and possibly the use of the parsonage house and garden. Much higher salaries could, however, be paid under exceptional circumstances. The rector of Haseby, for instance, was 'excused from residence by an Act of Parliament [he was Dean of Windsor], but his curate resides constantly in the parsonage house, and has a salary of sixty pounds per an. allowed him by Act of Parliament'.

Yorkshire and Nottinghamshire. Once again these returns illustrate that curates' stipends fluctuated enormously. The curate of Armthorpe near Doncaster received £27 6s. plus all the surplice fees; at Bardsey he got £30; but at Birstall near Pontefract only £10. Ralph Jackson reported from West Ayton that the impropriator, Cholmley Turner, allowed him no more than £13 6s. 8d.; which stood out in strong contrast with the £40 paid by the vicar of Northallerton to one of his two curates. Thomas Denton, who served Kirk Bramwith for a non-resident and debt-ridden rector, complained bitterly of his sad lot. His stipend was £30, but out of that, he reported, 'the rector stops four guineas as a rent for the parsonage house and the premises, tho' all the proceeding curates had these things rent-free: In short, what with reductions for rent, for repairing the house, premises and crossing a river, with which the parish is bounded; my annual income is not above twenty pounds clear: Which inconveniences are so sinking, that unless I have speedy redress from your Grace, which I humbly crave at present, my necessitous circumstances will oblige me to quit the curacy before Christmas next.' Curates were constantly on the move, seeking to better themselves and rarely remaining long in one place unless it were a good one or, as not infrequently happened, they were unable to find anything more suitable. Consequently they had little interest in the parishes they temporarily served, which suffered accordingly. Stephen Sutton, vicar of Kirkby-Ireleth drew the archbishop's attention to 'the irregularities of the lawless curate' of Broughton chapel, which included 'his keeping a publick Ale-house, his marrying of persons without any due publications of banns or a licence to do so and likewise at uncanonical hours' in order to add to his income and so help to support a large family'. Continuing in more general terms Sutton reported 'that a whole colony of poor raw boys taken from the home-bred insignificant schools of this county and ordained deacons on some sorry titles, mere Readers' places by his Lordship of Chester, hath (after some small probation here) been transported or sent abroad into your Grace's diocese within these five years, to seek their fortunes there, and furnish the Yorkshire clergy with low-priced curates. How the laity my countrymen will digest them I cannot tell, but I am apt to think they will make no great improvement under such weak teachers, either as to the honesty of their morals, or their better knowledge of religion and true virtue.' Not all Yorkshire curates however were unworthy of their parishioners' esteem. The people of Bransby informed the archbishop : 'being fully satisfied with the conduct of our present curate (Henry Bond); thought convenient to make our addresses to your Grace to desire you to prevail with Mr. Thompson the Rector to allow him more than five and twenty pound a year, for the support of himself and his family. We are certain that he may very well afford to do it; because his preferments are very considerable. And we do not offer this to your Grace's consideration with any design to oppose Mr. Thompson in any respect; but to redress the grievances which have hitherto happen'd by the too frequent removals of our curates.' Leonard Thompson, who was making as much as £250 out of his two livings of Bransby and Terrington, strongly resisted this demand. He told the archbishop that the twenty-five pounds plus surplice fees that he was giving Mr. Bond constituted 'more than any person of my acquaintance allows his curate out of a living of equal value'. Indeed he pitied 'the poor man's ill-judgement in order to raise his fortune', which was a scurvy enough return for 'my charitable intention in preserving him and his family from starving'.

The starving curate was not uncommon. Swift drew a true picture from life when he wrote of :

> Thy curate's place, thy fruitful wife,
> Thy busy, drudging scene of life,

> Thy insolent, illiterate vicar,
> Thy want of all consoling liquor,
> Thy threadbare gown, thy cassock rent,
> Thy credit sunk, thy money spent,
> Thy week made up of fasting days,
> Thy grate unconscious of a blaze,
> And to complete thy other curses,
> The quarterly demands of nurses,
> Are ills you wisely wish to leave,
> And fly for refuge to the grave.

Another of his poems was about the Reverend Robert Hewit, one of those galloping curates who rushed from church to church of a Sunday feverishly seeking to pick up a few extra shillings to balance the budget:

> I marched three miles through scorching sand,
> With zeal in heart and notes in hand;
> I rode four more to great St. Mary,
> Using four legs, when two were weary:
> To three fair virgins I did tie men,
> In the close bands of pleasing Hymen;
> I dipp'd two babes in holy water,
> And purified their mother after.
> Within an hour and eke a half,
> I preached three congregations deaf;
> Where, thundering out with lungs long-winded,
> I chopp'd so fast that few there minded.
> My emblem, the labourious sun,
> Saw all these mighty labours done
> Before one race of his was run.
> All this performed by Robert Hewit:
> What mortal else could e-er go through it.

As the century wore on and the value of benefices increased through grants from Queen Anne's Bounty, the benefits derived from enclosure, and other sources, the curate's financial position likewise improved. By an Act passed in 1796, 36 George III c. 83., the bishops were empowered to award a maximum stipend of £75 to curates serving the parishes of non-resident pluralists; but nothing was said about a minimum stipend, and no provision was made for cases where the incumbent was resident and employed an assistant. Indeed the average income by 1800 was no more than £56 to £60, and even as late as 1830 a parliamentary paper records that out of 4,254 curates, 1,631 still received salaries of no more than £60, although prices had risen considerably in the last thirty years.

The difficulties of a curate, with no private means and no social or political strings to pull, in securing a living were enormous; and most of them remained in that humble station all their lives until old age or sickness deprived them of their employment and they were cast upon the world to starve. At the age of fifty-eight the Reverend William Bickerstaffe, under master of the Lower Free Grammar School at Leicester and curate of the neighbouring villages of Great Wigston and Aylestone, approached the Lord Chancellor on 10 August 1786 concerning the benefice of St. Nicholas, Leicester, then vacant and in his lordship's gift. 'At fifty-eight years of age,' he wrote, 'permit a poor curate, unsupported by private property, to detain your attention a few moments. From 1750 I have been usher at the Free Grammar-school here, with an appointment of £19 16s. 0d. a year; seven years curate of St. Mary's my native parish, this borough; then six years curate at St. Martin with All Saints.' He went on to beg for St. Nicholas, which his headmaster, Mr. Pigott, was shortly to relinquish; not indeed a great prize but one that was dear to his heart. 'It is simply £35 a year; but as this corporation grants an annual aid to each living in Leicester of £10 a year St. Nicholas, joined to my school, might render me comfortable for life, and prevent the uncertainty of a curacy, and the hard necessity, at my time of life, of being harassed, in all weathers, by a distant cure.' Time dragged on and nothing was done. Bickerstaffe wrote to a friend: 'At 58 years of age, having more inclination to a church living than a wife, I applied to my old neighbour and play-fellow, Dr Farmer (Master of Emmanuel College, Cambridge) to procure me St Nicholas parish here . . . the living is not yet disposed of; the Lord Chancellor is, or lately was, at Buxton, and I remain uninformed of anything further: there is no room to expect a smile of favour till the gout is more civil. It seems like a chancery-suit. The present Lord Chancellor is said to be a leisurely gentleman in these matters. He keeps livings in suspense. . . . At my age I could tell him with strict propriety, "Bis dat, qui cito".' Three years after the date of his first application Bickerstaffe died, still unbeneficed. His obituary notice in *The Gentleman's Magazine* contained the ironical passage: 'His case had been lately laid before the Lord Chancellor, from whom there is reason to think some preferment would have been bestowed upon him had he lived.' The more influential William Bagshaw Stevens, headmaster of Repton, chaplain at Foremark, the Derbyshire home of Sir Robert Burdett, and the friend of Thomas Coutts, the banker, also had a deep longing for 'an independence', i.e. a good living, which like Bickerstaffe he found almost impossible to acquire. Through Coutts he bombarded the Lord Chancellor, the Crown and the bishop applying for vacant benefices; but it was only towards the very end of his comparatively short life that he secured the two small parishes of Seckington and Kingsbury in Warwickshire although in the course of less than ten years, 1792–1800, he had asked for more than twenty. He wrote to Thomas Coutts in March 1795: 'For some time to come I shall be a very Death-Watch among the Ancient Incumbents'; and added in his journal: 'Winter with all its horrors is again come upon us. . . . How this will agree with ancient incumbents, I know not.' Alas, they withstood its rigours far better than he had hoped. 'Old Edward was here the other evening as blithe as a bird and as tight as a drum.'

In the 1720s appeared a pamphlet, in the form of a letter addressed to the bishop of London, Edmund Gibson, written by the Reverend Thomas Stockhouse and entitled: *The Miseries and Great Hardships of the Inferior Clergy in and about London.* This made four pleas on behalf of poor curates: 'As we are the ministers of the most high God, we think we have the right to honour and respect; as our labour and time is entirely devoted to His service a right to maintenance and support; because the passions of men are not to be trusted, and that maintenance may not be precarious, a right to some legal security for it; because offences will come and that the weakest may not be undone, a right to justice and impartiality when we appeal.' Alas, none of these demands were at present met. The rector or vicar, however illiterate, idle or vicious, who 'lives in the great house' is honoured and fawned upon, whereas the 'little starved curate that lodges in a garret', who does all the work of the parish and is often a man of wit and learning, is regarded as a matter of course with contempt and derision, in which the incumbent himself set a disgraceful example : 'Mighty rectors riding over the heads of their readers and curates; receiving them with an air of superiority that would better become a Persian Monarch than a christian priest; breaking jests upon their poverty, and making themselves merry with their misfortunes; turning them among the herd of their servants, into the kitchen, 'till dinner comes in, and then shewing them what a mighty favour it is that they are permitted to sit down at the lower end of the table among their betters; curtailing in the meanwhile their allowances, which are only held at the will of their lord; keeping them under the worst of torments, a merciless suspense, and perpetual incertitude of daily bread; then turning them out at a minute's warning, purely to show the arbitrariness of their sway; and if at any time they pretend to murmur or complain, persecuting them with fury and revenge, and calling in a superior power to crush them.'

Canon Law, which provided for the curate's proper maintenance and protection, was systematically evaded. For instance, the demand that all curates must be licensed by the bishop was all too frequently ignored. An incumbent would say complaisantly to himself : ' 'Tis but my forgetting (as it were) to give my curate a nomination to the bishop, and then he can have no licence; he himself will not dare demand one of me; and if he does I cashier him at once, and the bishop is too much of a gentleman and my friend to call upon me for one or to insist upon such trifling niceties. While therefore I keep him from a licence (and that I will endeavour to do as long as I live) he's properly no curate of the place; and therefore I'll use him as I please : I will pay him as I please and send him adrift when I please, in spite of his boasted Act for the better Maintenance of Curates.' This statute of 1713, as has already been noted, had provided for a salary of £50 as a maximum, which should not fall below £20 as a minimum; but few curates ever reached the maximum, and even in London, where the cost of living was high, the stipend rarely rose above £30 per annum. Out of this a single man had to pay for board and lodgings, clothes and laundry, besides extras like books and 'something for charity and relief of the poor'. A married man, of course, was infinitely worse off since he had also to meet the requirements of a wife and growing family. Consequently it was no uncommon sight to 'see a Man of God with his shoes out of toes and his stockings out of heels, wandering about in an old russet coat or a tattered gown'. What a pitiable figure he cut in the pulpit, 'with a short gown . . . with a standing collar and sleeves straight at the hands to hide his want of linen'. A bricklayer or carpenter, who earned 2s. a day, was better off than he; most certainly 'any common footman, with seven pounds yearly, and seven shillings a week board-wages, with a good entire livery, his master's cast-off clothes, and now and then some accidental vails [tips]'.

The curate's study was usually no more than 'a little hole in the garret, with a stool and a table and a shelf'; his library a few dog-eared and torn theological books and classics; and his mind continually preyed upon by thoughts of unpaid bills. How indeed could he possibly be expected to turn out first-rate sermons or preach them without embarrassment when the church was full of his creditors and those upon whom he was dependent for financial assistance. But his chief grievance was that of insecurity. For all too many curates were kept unlicensed and so were liable to dismissal at a moment's notice. The bishops alone could protect them. 'We desire,' they exclaimed, 'to be examined by them

16. Sydney Smith, the curates' friend.

17. 'The curate of the parish returned from duty.' From an engraving published in 1793.

18. Bringing tithes to the vicar, 1793.

19. 'The Parsonage' by Thomas Rowlandson.

before we be admitted to any trust for fear of insufficiency, to have our allowances taxed and determined by them for fear of disagreements; to have a letter of licence under our own hand and seal for fear of collusion or removes; and no cause of dismission allowed against us but such as their own wisdom and impartiality upon proper hearing shall approve.' Above all a curate ought not to be removed, as all too frequently happened, 'upon the demise of one incumbent and the induction of another'. In a word they desired to be 'fixed permanently in a church where we have an unalienable right to serve as long as any curate is kept upon the place and the bishop is pleased to abide by his licence and approve of our service'. According to canon 137 every curate was expected to exhibit his licence at the very next episcopal visitation after his admission to a curacy. But in practice this rarely happened, since he had never been properly licensed and so remained during the term of his service at the mercy of his employer. Consequently he either became grossly subservient, 'to cringe and fawn and run and fly', or else displayed a gross carelessness in the discharge of his duties on the assumption : "I have no licence, and may therefore be dismissed by the Doctor this moment. His humour and mine may soon disagree and then I must be gone. . . . The parish was never committed to me, nor am I responsible for their souls. I'll do their offices, however perfunctorily, read them prayers and preach them sermons, and go to their sick, if they please to send for me, but as for the great pastoral care of their souls, let him look to that, he has undertook it and has the pay for it. The little pittance I have is sufficiently earned in what I do.' What was the remedy? Thomas Stockhouse boldly advocated the strike weapon. Let curates combine, strike, and if necessary seek for secular employment. They could scarcely be worse off than they were at present. 'Never serve,' they were advised, 'in the capacity of curates without proper faculty and designation from the bishop . . . you have their [the incumbents'] idleness, as well as multiplicity of livings, for your security, that they cannot do without you.' But, alas, there was also a multiplicity of curates and a pool of unemployed clergy searching continually for jobs; so such a rebellion never got off the ground!

The letter concluded with a number of more reasonable suggestions ranging from the better supervision of curates by their bishops, the reduction of pluralities in order to provide more benefices for them, and even allowing parishioners to have some say in the choice of their ministers, to permitting curates, when necessary, to undertake secular employments in order to eke out their stipend, to ensure that such a stipend was adequate for the provision of books and suitable clothing, to treat them on a social equality with incumbents, and to try and persuade patrons of livings to promote only the deserving. ' 'Tis telling patrons,' he exhorted Gibson, 'that, in disposing of livings, they should break through everything, the solicitations of the great, the sense of services and ties of consanguinity to come at the man of real worth, tho' he has never a friend in the world to make intercession for him.'

Yet little or nothing was done either to remedy these grievances or meet these demands, since at the very end of the century the poor curate of Broxbourne, William Jones, was still lamenting from personal experience : 'your "mastermen", who do their duty by proxy, haggling with poor curates, till they can find those who will starve with the fewest symptoms of discontent.' 'Those,' he went on, 'who court this genteel profession, with no other prospect but of being "journeymen", "soles" not "upper-leathers", which is (being interpreted) poor curates. They are truly to be pitied. If they regard present circumstances without "having respect unto recompence of the future", they would, I am sure, do better for themselves and for their families, by making interest for upper-servants' places in a genteel family, than by being mere "soles or understrappers" in the Church.' Jones himself augmented his own slender stipend by keeping a small school; but even so he had considerable difficulty in making both ends meet. He recorded ruefully in his journal on Easter Day 1784 : 'Providence seems

114

now to frown on me, to blast all my schemes. An increasing family and a decreasing income. What is to be done? . . . I will not despair. The prospect will presently lighten. It struck a damp on my spirits yesterday, when on casting up my accounts, I found that the expenses of the last quarter exceeded £36, which sum is almost double my income for the same quarter.' None the less he was an extremely conscientious parish priest. 'I am now,' he wrote, on 29 June 1799, 'in the nineteenth year of my servitude [i.e. curateship] . . . and to the very best of my recollection or my clerk's, two or at the most three Sundays are all that I have ever been absent from my parish in all that time.' He visited his people regularly, especially the sick, and, despite his own poverty, helped his needy neighbours financially. But, as a mere curate, he did not always win the respect and affection he deserved. He told his particular enemy, the farmer Mr. Rogers, 'I am sorry to feel towards any creature, which a good and gracious God has made, such sentiments as are excited in my breast towards you, by the gross ill-usage which I have experienced from you.' Others could be equally hurtful. 'After tapping, for some time, at Dame Peake's door, old nurse Hobbs opened it just enough to put her head out, and to tell me that I was not to enter. "She is not bad enough for you, Sir".' Even his own servants would not obey his orders. A mere chit of a skivvy, Miss Crouch the shoe-cleaner, aged fifteen, defied him and refused to go to bed before midnight. Above all, those very parishioners for whom he worked himself to the bone exhibited a strange reluctance to pay the clerical dues they owed him. Some refused them outright and others, as he remarked, 'pay them very partially and I may add, "grudgingly and of necessity".' Rogers actually tried to stop him from succeeding to the benefice when that fell vacant in 1801 by writing letters to the patron, the Bishop of London, 'full of calumnies and misrepresentations'; but fortunately in vain. His family life was not a happy one, with a nagging shrew of a wife, Theodosa, a real scold, whose tantrums compelled her husband to keep 'A Book of Domestic Lamentations'; nine children to support; and living in a tumbledown vicarage on a tiny stipend. Yet he was a cheerful man, blessed with good health, an equitable temperament, a sense of humour and a patient disposition. His clothes were shabby and stained with snuff, to which 'filthy worse than beastly practice' he was addicted. He was last in bed at night and the first out in the morning; his family despised him and failed even to celebrate his birthday; and his pupils were often troublesome and sometimes non-existent. He loaned money to friends which he could ill-afford and worried whether he would ever get it back again; he kept a coffin in his study and contemplated from his bedroom window the yew-tree under which he hoped to be buried. But nothing could quench his love of life, of good food and drink, and of social occasions like weddings and funerals. We see him at his happiest alone in his study, where with his beloved books, the draught from the chimney at length blocked, and his knees unbuttoned, he took his ease. 'How happy, how very happy,' he wrote in his journal, 'do I feel myself in my dear little room . . . I am undisturbed. I have my cheerful little fire, my books and in short every comfort which I can reasonably desire. I read, I reflect, I write, and I endeavour to enjoy as far as I can that blessed leisure and absence of care with which the good Providence of my Heavenly Father has indulged me.' Jones died on 21 October 1821 in the sixty-seventh year of his age.

Not all curates, however, were down-trodden, poverty-stricken and unsuccessful. The Reverend John Willan, curate of St. Peter-at-the-Arches in Lincoln from January 1751–2 until his death in 1778, has left behind him a memorandum and account book, which record the income from his curacies and other professional employments, the profits of his small estate in Westmorland, and his transactions as an investor, besides his household and other expenses. Willan, who came of yeoman stock, was certainly a hard-headed and successful business man. His curacy brought him in about £51, to which he could add a further £10 of private income. But apart from officiating at St. Peter's he rode five miles each Sunday morning to preach at Reepham, for which he received a fee of 7s. 6d. Occasionally he deputised for his rector, Gilbert Benet, who was sheriff's chaplain, and preached the Assize Sermon that earned him another 17s. 6d.; while he also took duty at the castle gaol for £1 5s. He lodged with the local saddler, Mr. Mason, to whom he paid £15 per annum for board and lodging. He spent his money wisely: dressing well, always wearing spotless linen and highly polished boots, and making a point of being regularly shaved; whereby he ensured for himself the respect of his fashionable congregation. In 1759 he married the mayor of Lincoln's daughter, Sarah Obbinson, who brought with her a modest dowry. Willan's professional income now rapidly increased to about £85 per annum, which included yet another assistant curacy at St. Swithin, Lincoln, and £13 from the chaplaincy of the gaol. But to this he also added substantially through a variety of secular employments: buying and selling goods of all kinds, systematic betting and card-playing, and a flourishing money-lending business. As a result he and his wife lived very comfortably in a well-furnished rented house, dressed well and entertained modestly. They employed a servant at 30s. a year, books were plentiful and the curate's sermons continued to be appreciated by an intelligent and discerning congregation. On the other side of the ledger it must be recorded that his charitable gifts were not remarkable either for their size or number.

Another equally successful curate was Henry Mease, Fellow of Jesus College, Oxford, who became 'officiating minister' at Cheltenham in 1709; and later held the curacies of Staverton, Boddington Chapel and St. Michael, Bristol, from 1716 to 1719. In addition he served as afternoon lecturer in Cheltenham from 1710 until 1723; and, having obtained the bishop's licence to teach, set up his own school during 1719. His total income from all sources in 1710 amounted to £61 18s. 2d., which included the 'profits' of his Fellowship, £18, and the preacher's fee of £3 4s. 6d. at Great St. Mary's, Oxford. At that date the combined value of the Cheltenham curacy and lectureship was

£40 1s. 8d.; but by 1713 this income had risen to £95 10s. After November in that year he lost his Fellowship, but by now had amassed sufficient capital to be able to loan money at a high rate of interest, which eventually enabled him to acquire seven mortgages worth £900. His curacies at Staverton and Boddington yielded £105 8s. 6d. between 1716 and 1719, while that of St. Michael's, Bristol, brought him in a steady £49 12s. per annum; no inconsiderable income. We have no record of what he earned from school fees, but since the establishment flourished exceedingly these must have been substantial. In connection with this last he also engaged in a certain amount of subsistence farming: rearing pigs and poultry, and growing corn and beans. In 1724 he was appointed to the rectory of Alderton, yet continued to live and run his school in Cheltenham until 1738 when he was instituted to the more important benefice of Swindon. He died in 1746. Mease, who was a bachelor, lived very comfortably, if not luxuriously. He dressed well, sometimes elegantly, wore expensive wigs, ate and drank always of the best, smoked and took snuff a good deal, was constantly making journeys by coach or on horse-back to such places as Oxford, London, Abergavenny, Gloucester and Bristol, where he invariably put up at the best inns, and was extremely generous to relations, servants and charities. His house in Cheltenham was a large and comfortable one, which required a window-tax of 20s a year, its furnishings were of the highest class, and it possessed a pleasant garden. He employed a jobbing gardener and at least one female servant to whom he paid an average wage of £2 10s. per annum, plus a bonus of 10s. 6d. at Christmas. Here then was no clerical 'journeyman' or 'understrapper', but a prosperous, contented, highly-respected and learned gentleman, who could modestly claim to have made a success of his profession long before he had acquired his first living.

But the best example of all well-to-do curates in the eighteenth century is probably that of James Woodforde, who while still a Fellow of New College, Oxford, served various curacies, especially those of Ansford and Castle Cary in Somerset of which his father, Samuel Woodforde, was the incumbent. On 2 May 1763 the diarist wrote: 'Sale spoke to me this morning concerning the curacy of Newton-Purcell, which I have promised him to take and serve the Sunday after Trinity Sunday; it is about 20 miles from Oxford; and I am to receive per annum for serving it, besides surplice fees, £28. I am only to serve it during Mr. Sale's Proctorship.' That summer he also did duty at a number of other villages in the vicinity before leaving Oxford on 12 September for Somerset, where in October he became curate of Thurloxton and lodged with Squire Cross at a cost of £21 a year. The stipend was £40. Here he recorded a typical Sunday on 6 November: 'Breakfasted, dined, supp'd and laid at Mr. Cross's. Read prayers and preached this morning at my church of Thurloxton, it being Sunday. I likewise read prayers there this afternoon. After the afternoon service, I privately baptised Mrs. Cross's late [i.e. lately born] child which was a boy, and by the name of Richard, in Mrs. Cross's bedroom in this house. One Farmer Major, of this parish, spent the afternoon and evening here, drinking with Mr. Cross all the time, neither of them ate any supper, and I left them drinking when I went to bed, which was about 10.' Soon afterwards he left Thurloxton for a curacy at Babcary a few miles away, where he was to take two services per Sunday in return for a salary of £30, plus the use of the parsonage. There on 22 June 1764 he gave a lavish bachelor's supper party, and later the guests 'plaid at fives in Babcary churchyard this evening, and I lost there with Mr. Lewis Bower at betting with him 0–1–6'. As always he was very generous to his parishioners: 'December 24 . . . The new singers came very late this evening and they sang a Cristmas carol and an anthem and they had cyder as usual and 0–2–0. . . . Dec. 25. Fifteen poor old people dined here as usual being Xmas day.' On the other hand he could be stern enough when the situation required it: 'April 7. 1765. My clarke Sam Hutchins sat up all last night drinking therefore he did not attend at the Holy Sacrament (Easter Day) for which I gave him a severe lecture and he promised me never to be guilty of the same again.' Soon afterwards his father lost his Castle Cary curate and the diarist took over, but still retained Babcary, where on 11 July he gave a dinner party to fourteen gentlemen, 'one of whom was not invited', and they played ball in the churchyard. That autumn, however, he finally relinquished Babcary and became his father's full-time curate, living with his brother John, who was a bit of a playboy, in the Lower House at Ansford which belonged to his mother.

Despite the fact that he lived and acted like a country gentleman he was deeply religious and carried out his clerical duties most conscientiously, although there were occasional lapses: 'Oct. 18. 1766. I entirely forgot that this was St. Luke's Day, and therefore did not read prayers at C. Cary which I should have done otherwise. As it was not done wilfully I hope God will forgive it.' He visited the sick and dying most assiduously and on one occasion at least compelled an erring Castle Cary girl to perform a public penance in church. Yet he did not allow his profession to interfere in any way with his pleasures: playing games and betting on them, dancing all hours, shooting and fishing, attending plays and cockfights, entertaining and being entertained by his well-to-do neighbours, when he partook of gargantuan meals and drank an enormous amount of wine. He was indeed to remain a bachelor all his days but that did not prevent him from enjoying the company of pretty girls. On 16 February 1767 he took a certain Miss Jordan 'to a concert and ball' at the 'Bear' in Wincanton, when he danced every dance with her from 10 p.m. to 4 a.m. And he fell in love for a time with Betsey White of Shepton, although nothing ultimately came of it.

He was very fond of animals and clever at doctoring them: 'Oct. 26, 1768. I had a poor little cat, that had one of her ribs broke and that laid across her belly, and we could not tell what it was, and she in great pain. I therefore with a small pen knife this morning opened one side of her and took it out, and performed the operation very well and afterwards sewed it up and put Friars Balsam to it. . . . It grieved me much to see the poor creature in such pain before, and therefore made me undertake the above which I hope will preserve the life of the poor creature.' He was also very good with horses. But he was not without his difficulties at Castle Cary. The squire, Justice Creed, wished to demolish the church gallery because the choir had denied one of his men access to it; and the parish was up in arms. Woodforde refused to take sides and eventually arranged a compromise whereby the gallery was preserved but partitioned, one part being reserved for the choir and the other open to the public. The diarist himself, however, had his own troubles with his choir: 'Nov. 12, 1769. I read prayers and preached this morning in C. Cary church. I was disturbed this morning at Cary church by the singers. I sent my clerk some time back to the Cary singers to desire that they would not sing the responses in the communion service, which they complied with for several Sundays, but this morning after the first commandment they had the impudence to sing the response, and therefore I spoke to them out of my desk, to say and not to sing the responses which they did after, and at other places they sang as usual.' For the moment all was well, but a fortnight later the entire choir absented themselves, 'being highly affronted with me at what I lately had done'. No wonder Woodforde remarked ruefully: 'Great and many are the divisions in C. Cary, and some almost irreconcilable. Send us Peace O Lord! With Thee O Lord all things are possible.' But by Christmas the curate and his singers were reunited and they received their usual cider and 2s.

The diarist was a devoted son and a great comfort to his father in his last illness. 'Better parents no children ever had than we have been blessed with,' he wrote, 'blessed be God for it and make us more worthy than we are for all thy goodness to us.' He was encouraged both by the patron and the Bishop of Bath and Wells to hope that he would succeed his father in the two livings, and on the strength of this moved into Ansford parsonage, but it was not to be. His cousin, Frank Woodforde, was appointed to Ansford and a Mr. Wickham to Castle Cary. No love was lost between the two branches of the Woodforde family, so the diarist decided to relinquish his curacies and return to Oxford. This decision was hastened by the unkind behaviour of his cousin : 'July 19, 1773, Mr. Frank Woodforde was this morning inducted into the living of Ansford, and he immediately sent me a line that he intends serving Ansford next Sunday himself, which notice of my leaving the curacy is I think not only unkind but very ungentlemanlike. I must be content. Far be it from me to expect any favour at all from that House. All their actions to-wards me are bad. . . . I intend to quit the parsonage house when my year is up, and which will be Lady Day next, and to take up my residence once more at New College.' This he did; and not long afterwards, on 15 December 1774, was voted into the college living of Weston Longueville in Norfolk, where he was to remain for the rest of his life.

Another well-to-do curate was William Sellon, who died in 1780, when he was deriving over a thousand pounds a year from various posts in London, which included the curateship of the united parishes of St. James and St. John, Clerkenwell, the position of joint evening preacher at the Magdalen Chapel, and the alternate afternoon lectureship at St. Andrew's, Holborn, and St. Giles-in-the-Fields.

In contrast to such men there appeared in the latter half of the century the enthusiastic evangelical curate, a product of the Religious Revival. Few Anglican curates in the eighteenth century were influenced by the older Non-conformist sects, whom they either viewed with suspicion and abhorrence or else were prepared to extend to them no more than a patronising tolerance. But some were swept off their feet by the Methodists. In the 1740s, for example, when David Taylor was building up the first Wesleyan society in Sheffield, he was greatly assisted by the Reverend Mr. Dodge, curate of the Ecclesall Chapel, who, we are told, 'frequently wept over his auditors while enforcing the great truths of the Gospel'; but at the cost of raising up many enemies among the more orthodox members of the Establishment.

Down in Cornwall Samuel Walker, curate of Truro, the acknowledged leader of the evangelical clergy of those parts during the '50s, who founded a famous clerical club and became a noted parish priest and revivalist, was also for a time closely associated with the Methodists. He welcomed both John and Charles Wesley into his parish and freely corresponded with them. However he eventually parted company with them over the whole question of the appointment of lay-preachers and their use in supervising the newly founded Wesleyan societies that were springing up everywhere, and which, in Walker's opinion, at any rate in Evangelical parishes, ought to have been handed over to the care of the incumbent. In fact he went so far as to accuse Wesley of seeking to set up 'a Church within a Church' or even of outright 'Separation'. Walker indeed clearly foresaw that it would ultimately become impossible for the Wesleys to retain their organisation within the Church of England, and he wisely withdrew in time, whilst striving with all his might and main to achieve the same spiritual results through a 'regular', disciplined and devoted Anglican ministry.

Another Anglican evangelical of Walker's type was the Reverend Thomas Jones, who for forty years, from 1785 to 1828, was the ill-paid curate of the little Northamptonshire village of Creaton. Jones was ordained in 1774 and served various curacies in Wales and western England, where he acquired his evangelical principles; but these so offended his employers that he was dismissed again and again. At Oswestry the rural dean even tried the expedient of beating him about the head with a stick in order to get rid of his theological views. Eventually, through the influence of Charles Simeon, one of the leaders of the Revival, he was appointed to Creaton, where he remained for the rest of his life. Creaton had already experienced an awakening under the previous curate, Abraham Maddock, who had laboured there for thirteen years; and Jones merely extended and enlarged the work. People flocked to hear him from neighbouring villages. He held two full services each Sunday and a lecture on Wednesday evenings, while in 1789 he started the first Sunday school in the county. When Jones first went to Creaton he received no more than £25 per annum; but from 1810 onwards he was also curate of the neighbouring village of Spratton and his salary rose to £60. Since there was no parsonage Jones lodged at an inn, with the permission of the bishop. From the profits of his writings he established parochial clubs to help the sick and poor, employed a woman to teach girls to sew, and built a row of houses for elderly widows. He was a strong supporter of the annual clerical meeting of like-minded evangelical clergy, which used to meet at Creaton on Easter Tuesday for a sermon and discussion, until in 1804 the Bishop of Peterborough put a stop to the preaching. Outside his parishes he was the founder of various societies, notably one for the Relief of Poor Pious Clergymen, and a Clerical Education Society for the training of ordinands. He was also associated with the founding of the Bible Society. As a writer he became famous for translating evangelical works into Welsh. From 1828 to 1833 he was rector of Creaton, but then retired in favour of the patron's son. Towards the end of his life he went blind, and died in 1845.

For the ideal eighteenth-century curate in literature we must turn to Henry Fielding's Abraham Adams, who, despite the fact that he possessed a wife and six children, and at the age of fifty was earning no more than £23 a year, was an excellent scholar and a humble, fearless christian; one who was always prepared to defend the poor and needy against their oppressors. When for instance Lady Booby threatened to report him to his rector and get him dismissed for harbouring vagabonds in the parish, he replied with dignity: 'Madam, I am in the service of a Master who will never discard me for doing my duty; and if the Doctor (for indeed I have never been able to pay for a licence) thinks proper to turn me from my cure, God will provide me, I hope, another. At least my family, as well as myself, have hands; and

He will prosper, I doubt not, our endeavours to get our bread honestly with them. Whilst my conscience is pure, I shall never fear what man can do unto me.'

Any curate, in fact, who had the courage to step out of line, soon found himself in trouble. The Reverend Samuel May, curate of Roborough, Devon, was charged by his churchwardens in 1765 with quitting his church one Sunday morning during divine service and entering the public house 'to search if there were any people in the publick house instead of in church'; and also, at the evening service, of leaving his desk after the second lesson and ordering all strangers to vacate the building. When they were slow to do so, 'he violently laid hold and pulled and pushed them out'. May in his defence declared that for many years on Revel Sunday, i.e. when a church ale was being held, he had been plagued by drunken and riotous non-parishioners, most of them 'young, giddy and most abandoned creatures of all the neighbouring parishes', who invaded his church in service time, laughing, talking, running from seat to seat, and fighting among themselves. On one occasion two drunks had staged a boxing match in the middle of the aisle while he was preaching; and on another a man was so intoxicated that he rolled about on the floor until his wig fell off. The curate therefore felt justified in clearing both public house and church of these undesirable strangers; but he strongly denied, and produced witnesses to prove it, that he had never assaulted anyone. None the less he had clearly overstepped his authority, his excuses were swept aside, and he was severely admonished and ordered to pay the costs of the suit.

In Samuel Wesley's *Letter to a Curate* we are given a picture of the ideal type of eighteenth-century curate : he must visit from house to house, read prayers on Sundays and holy days, recite the Litany on Wednesdays and Fridays, teach his people to sing the metrical psalms, preach a good sermon, catechise the young, persuade all parents to bring their children to church for baptism, celebrate communion at least once a month, see that all his parishioners come regularly to church, and insist on exacting penances for breaches of church discipline. He himself must never enter a public house, and try and restrain his church-wardens from doing likewise, except in the way of duty; but above all let him beware of public disputations with Dissenters, who 'will always out-face and out-lung you'. 'Go on,' Wesley concluded, 'in the way of duty. I hope there will be no dispute between us, but who shall run fastest and fairest.'

NOTE. See appendix for an example of the difficulties experienced by the congregation of a chapel of ease in securing a stipend for a curate.

CHAPTER VI

The Nineteenth-Century Curate

The Act of 1796, 36 George III c. 83., had raised the maximum curate's stipend to £75, plus the use of the parsonage house or, if the house was not included, an additional £15. But nothing was said about a minimum stipend, and judging from those paid in the Oxford diocese at the beginning of the new century these figures were rarely reached. In 1799, for example, one curate was being paid £20, nineteen between £20 and £29, sixteen between £50 and £59, and only one the full maximum of £75. However, many of the poorer-paid curates were either doing duty in more than one parish, possessed college chaplaincies, or taught in a school, whereby their salaries were considerably augmented. The Reverend C. L. Kerby served the three parishes of Chinnor, Crowell and Emmington; the Reverend John Francis those of Westwell, Swinbrook and Shilton; while Lionel Lampett not only did duty at Duns Tew and Barford St. Michael, but held the mastership of Dr. Radcliffe's Grammar School at Steeple Aston. This last gentleman, we are told, continued to fulfil these functions 'till long after the infirmities of age had compelled him to travel in a sedan chair between two stalwart labourers'.

In all, some thirteen men were acting as curates to two or more parishes at this period in and around the city of Oxford. William Scott's Non-Residence Act was aimed at this sort of situation, since it made residence compulsory on all livings over the value of £300 and declared that the serving of more than two churches on any one Sunday could only be permitted with the express consent of the bishop. This measure, it was feared, would make many curates redundant, and Queen Anne's Bounty set up a relief office for those thrown out of work. But the Act was so weakly and hesitantly applied that very few curates were actually displaced, although some £8,000 was set aside for this charitable task. In 1804 eight men were helped by it, who were paid three-quarters of what they had previously been earning. But the Board went out of their way to make their unemployment less palatable than employment, 'and drove them back to stipendiary servitude'. After that they never had more than three curates on their hands at any one time. One curate at any rate did quite well out of this fund. His name was Edward Gillesby and he had been dismissed from a curacy at Blisworth in Northamptonshire. His bishop, Madan of Peterborough, continually backed his application, which at first was very generously met. In 1805 he was paid £52 10s., and a year later £40; in 1807 and 1808 he received £35 and £30 respectively; but by 1809 they were getting rather tired of him and cut him down to £25; finally they washed their hands of him altogether.

Between 1803 and 1813 the lords Percival and Harrowby made strenuous efforts to get a new Curates' Act through Parliament, which was finally passed in the latter year, 53 George III c. 149, and was confirmed in 1817, 57 George III c. 99, that laid down a minimum stipend of £80 to be paid with or without the consent of the incumbent; but in the case of large and wealthy livings must be raised to a maximum of £150. Curates, however, who were licensed to serve two adjoining parishes would suffer a reduction of £30 in the full amount of both stipends. These Acts were later reinforced by the Pluralities Act of 1838, 1 & 2 Vict. c. 106, which not only compelled incumbents to reside on their livings, but made the appointment of a curate compulsory in populous parishes or in benefices containing more than one church. Unfortunately these Acts only worked partially and made their effects felt very gradually, since the Parliamentary returns for the first half of the century reveal that many curates were still receiving stipends far below those awarded by law. As early as 1808 Sydney Smith wrote in *The Edinburgh Review*: 'Is it

20. Contrasts in preaching : brimstone and treacle.

21. Vicar riding to hounds with the local aristocracy; satirical drawing by Thomas Rowlandson 1821.

23. Preaching and praying in Victorian times.

22. Satirical drawing of a Victorian marriage ceremony.

24. 'The New Curate'; painting by Wynfield c. 1870.

25. Decorating the church; drawing by Leech.

possible to prevent a curate from pledging himself to his rector, that he will accept only half the legal salary, if he is so fortunate as to be preferred among a host of rivals, who are willing to engage on the same terms? You may make these contracts illegal : what then? Men laugh at such prohibitions; and they always become a dead letter. . . . The Law cannot arm clergyman against clergyman.'

From about 1820 onwards the reform both of Church and State was very much in the air; and certainly many curates, to the wrath of the more conservative and better-off clergy, began to agitate for it; so much so that in 1830 Sydney Smith wrote to Lady Holland : 'there is a strong impression that there will be a rising of Curates. Should anything of this kind occur they will be committed to hard preaching on the tread-pulpit (a new machine) and rendered incapable of ever hereafter collecting great or small tithes'. No such rising took place; but in 1837 appeared *A Curate's Views of Church Reform*, by the Reverend J. Jordan, which boldly asserted the equality of curate and incumbent, and demanded a drastic reform of the Church both in its temporalities and spiritualities, especially the abolition of pluralities. 'Now,' he wrote, 'I am both Deacon and Priest, and though in a temporal point of view I may be low, yet in a spiritual one I claim to be upon a level with all the rest, Bishops alone excepted.' Curates, he continued, must speak out; otherwise they could be accused of accepting the present system, and hoping, if generally vainly, ultimately to participate in its fruits. 'If under such imputation as this we are silent, we know that our silence must be construed as a confession of the truth of the charge.' The remedy was simple : the enormous wealth of archbishops, bishops, deans and chapters, and wealthy incumbents should be drastically reduced and provision made out of the proceeds for establishing an independent minister to every five hundred people.

No doubt the Ecclesiastical Commission, which was then sitting, took note of these radical suggestions, and acted upon some of them. But there were in fact too many subservient curates about

I

only too pleased to accept anything that was offered them, which would amount very often to no more than £50 per annum, and perhaps as little as £35, to make it possible to enforce a living minimum wage. These men were mostly the sons of poor parents of low social standing, who possessed no private means and would never become incumbents. Indeed, as likely as not, if they did not die in harness, they would be cast out to starve when they had passed their usefulness. The obituary notice of the Reverend Miles Parkin, curate of Aston Rowant, Stokenchurch, Chinnor and Crowell, ran as follows : 'In St. Luke's Ward, at St. Bartholomew's Hospital, the Reverend Mr. Parkin, late of Queen's College, Oxford. His distress and indigence were so great, having a wife and four children, that his illness, it is apprehended, was occasioned by the want of the common necessities of life.' Another curate, Thomas Nutt of Barford St. John and Bodicote, died at his cottage in the latter village during 1853 under very similar conditions. James Palmer, curate of Headington, wrote to a Balliol friend in 1806 : 'If I had been the 19th cousin of a lord I might have attained hopes of a living; but I have not one drop of Duke's blood in me that I know of, and have no-one to patronize or assist me, so that probably I shall continue a curate all my life.' In this particular case Mr. Palmer did not live long enough to find out, since he was thrown from his horse and killed in 1808. But most curates continued in servitude for the rest of a long ministry, their hearts gradually sickened by hope deferred.

The Curate Acts of 1813 and 1817, together with the Pluralities Act of 1838, gradually made their influence felt. During the 1820s for example, there were nineteen cases in the Oxford diocese of curates serving neighbouring churches, but the visitation returns of 1866 recorded only four. The advent of Bishop Samuel Wilberforce in this particular diocese indeed entirely changed the whole situation. He brought pressure to bear upon incumbents to appoint resident curates, and through the Diocesan Society, which was founded in 1832, made grants to supplement their stipends. Another feature of his episcopate was the rapid increase in the number of perpetual curacies in the bishop's gift, endowed either by the Diocesan Society or Queen Anne's Bounty, which enabled many curates to obtain security, independence and a reasonable living, i.e. £80 to £100 a year; but it also meant that they would get no higher up the clerical tree, and were now unable, like their predecessors, to supplement their income by outside work. To the comprehensive question in article 7 of the visitation returns 1854 : 'Does he [the curate] perform any other duty as incumbent, curate, lecturer, chaplain, master or assistant in any school?', no more than thirty-nine parishes replied in the affirmative.

Socially the average nineteenth-century curate acquired but little of that prestige which the better-off incumbent was now enjoying. His poverty, insecurity, plebeian birth and sometimes his uncouthness frequently led both his employer and parishioners to treat him either with contempt, ridicule or pity. Anthony Trollope wrote of him in 1866 as still living on £70 a year, doing three-quarters of the work of the parish, and gradually losing his first religious fervour : 'Gradually there creeps upon him the heart-breaking disappointment of a soured and injured man. In the midst of this he takes to himself a wife . . . enjoying at the moment a little fitful gleam of short-lived worldly pleasure . . . after that all collapses and he goes down into irrevocable misery and distress. In a few years we know him as a beggar of old clothes, as a man whom from time to time his friends are asked to lift from unutterable depths by donations which no gentleman can take without a crushed spirit—as a pauper whom the poor around him know to be a pauper and will not, therefore respect as a minister of their religion.'

Augustus Hare described in 1840 how the curates were treated at Stoke Rectory in Shropshire. They came to luncheon every Sunday, but were only admitted through the back door. During the meal they were not expected to speak; but afterwards had to give an account of their week's work to the rector's wife, Mrs. Leycester, and were 'soundly rated if their actions did not correspond with her intentions'. One of them, Martin Stow, actually had the audacity to fall in love with a daughter of the Hare family, who returned his affection; but their union was successfully prevented by her parents on the grounds that he was no more than 'a mere country curate'. Another curate, Henry Frost of Blather-wycke in Northamptonshire, when faced with a similar situation in relation to his squire, took the bull by the horns and eloped with his beloved, a Miss O'Brien. This story ended happily with Squire O'Brien accepting the situation and welcoming the runaways back into the bosom of the family.

Augustus Hare also recounted the tale of the unfortunate curate of St. Buryan's in Cornwall, whose non-resident rector, Mr. Stanhope, employed him at a ridiculously tiny salary because he was a harmless maniac. 'He used to be fastened to the Altar or the reading desk. When once there, he was quite sane enough to go through the service perfectly. On weekday evenings he earned his subsistence by playing the fiddle at village taverns.' George Eliot, on the other hand, has drawn for us in the person of the Reverend Amos Barton, curate of Shepperton, a much more generalised figure. Certainly it is not an unsympathetic portrait. Barton was paid in 1828 the not ungenerous salary of £80 a year by his absentee vicar and also inhabited the parsonage free of charge. He was an ardent evangelical, worked hard in the parish, restored the church which was in ruins, preached two extemporary sermons every Sunday at the workhouse besides his regular duty, and took weekday services in cottages. He took no holidays and his labours never ceased; but they failed to earn him the respect of his parishioners, who were more influenced by his poverty, that constantly ran him into debt, his shabby appearance, and lack of education and social standing. 'Rather a low-bred fellow, I think, Barton,' said Mr. Pilgrim, 'they say his father was a Dissenting shoemaker; and he's half a dissenter himself.' 'Well,' replied Mrs. Hacket, 'I think he's a good sort of man, for all he's not over-burden'd in the upper story.' The squire's daughter, Miss Julia Farquar, 'observed that she *never* heard anyone sniff so frightfully as Mr. Barton did. She had a great mind to offer him her pocket-handkerchief; and her sister, Arabella, 'wondered why he always said he was going for to do a thing'. Poor Amos! bad grammar, appalling clothes, plebeian habits, and an unfortunate way, when he laughed, of showing 'the remainder of a set of teeth, which, like the remnants of the Old Guard, were few in number, and very much the worse for wear'. His fellow clergy were equally critical. Mr. Fellowes, a neighbouring rector and magistrate, commented unkindly: 'Now *I* never liked Barton. He is not a gentleman. Why, he used to be on terms of intimacy with that canting Prior, who died a little while ago: a fellow who soaked himself with spirits, and talked of the Gospel through an inflamed nose.' Then, to crown all these insults, and despite his devoted service to the church and parish, he received a letter from his absentee vicar, Mr. Carpe, stating that he was coming to reside at Shepperton and giving his curate six months notice. This abrupt dismissal aroused some bitter feelings in Amos' breast since it quickly became apparent that this sudden determination to reside was no more than a pretext for getting rid of him in order to hand over the curacy to a brother-in-law. Neither was it easy to obtain a new situation; and in the end he was compelled to take a post in a large manufacturing town, 'where his walks would be among noisy streets and dingy alleys, and where the children would have no garden to play in, no pleasant farm-houses to visit'.

The Brontës at Haworth in Yorkshire had three curates, equally uncouth and enthusiastic, but of a Puseyite rather than an evangelical complexion. They used to rush uninvited into the rectory for tea, when poor Charlotte was hot and tired from her cooking and other domestic chores. 'I would have served them out their tea in peace,' she declared, 'but they began glorifying themselves and abusing dissenters in such a manner that my temper lost its balance, and I pronounced a few sentences sharply and rapidly, which struck them all dumb.' Her particular bug-bear was a certain Mr. Weighman, whom she christened 'Miss Celia Amelia', whose principal aim in life appeared to be to crush the local Baptists and Methodists, of whom the parish was full, by the fury of his attacks upon them from the pulpit. However, Charlotte herself succumbed to another curate, the Reverend A. B. Nicholls, a brilliant and conscientious clergyman, whose labours, especially for the National Sunday Schools, received the highest commendation : 'for uprightness and steadiness of conduct, activity in the prosecution of his pastoral labours, and especially successful management of the parochial schools, there is not to be found his equal.'

The notorious Parson John Froude of Knowstone in Devonshire is reliably reported to have made his wretched curate, whom he disliked and persecuted, drunk one Sunday between services; and then caused him to be hung up in an empty corn-sack from a beam in an out-house, while the church bell rang in vain for evensong, which the curate could not and the vicar would not take. If the average incumbent did not go as far as that, he none the less expected his curate to shoulder all the drudgery of the parish, paid him as little as possible and often treated him as little better than a superior servant. A pamphlet entitled *The Whole Case of the Unbeneficed Clergy*, published in 1843, by an anonymous presbyter, described the evils of the system. He indeed began by declaring that he was not one to 'countenance the michievous and vulgar error, that the Curates, so called do all or most of the work, while the incumbents do little or none'; but then went on to list the former's unhappy situation. His average income was in the region of £80 to £100, rising in a few cases to £120 or £150, when 'it is eagerly sought after by numerous applicants'; yet even these larger incomes barely sufficed for his needs, bearing in mind that he had to keep up some sort of appearance in the parish, entertain however simply, and subscribe to charity. Then, perforce, he was always on the move, since 'there is no situation so precarious as that of the unbeneficed clergy', despite the much vaunted protection supposed to be provided them by the bishop's licence. Such removals were expensive, had to be paid for out of their own pockets, and when they ultimately arrived in their new posts they were no better off or secure than heretofore. Moreover from the parish's point of view these migratory habits were highly undesirable, as a curate who is unsettled and probably in financial difficulties, is unlikely to be deeply interested in his work. 'He will not heartily enter into those various schemes or plans for doing good . . . he feels no encouragement to follow out the suggestions that may be made to him. Furthermore he is likely, in order to make ends meet, to engage in secular employments that will take up much of his time, particularly schoolmastering or private tuition.'

The Pluralities Act of 1838, later reinforced by the Pluralities Acts Amendment Act, 48 & 49 Vict. c. 54, 1885, and the Benefices Act 1898, 61 & 62 Vict. c. 48, had regulated the curate's stipend in the case of non-resident incumbents along the lines of £80 to £100 for a small country village, and £120, £135, and £150 for populations respectively of 500, 750 and over 1,000. Benefices of more than 2,000 souls were to be served by two curates. But, alas, no provision was made for an assistant in parishes where the incumbent resided, who could still pay what he pleased, i.e. an income sufficient to attract an applicant; and as the century drew on it was the resident incumbent rather than his non-resident brother who became the norm. In 1838, 3,078 curates were serving non-residents; but by 1864 this number had been reduced to 955 and grew steadily smaller. Consequently the average curate's position considerably worsened. 'Before Reform,' writes Professor Owen Chadwick, 'the curate often obtained a sole charge quickly, lived free in the parsonage house, and was independent. After Reform he competed for 7,000 adequate (over £200) livings with some 5,000 incumbents of inadequate livings and 5,000 other curates; and out of the 7,000 adequate livings many were family perquisites and not open to most curates.' The anonymous author of *The Whole Case of the Unbeneficed Clergy* suggested indeed as a remedy what he called the 'one-third rule', i.e. Parliament should pass a measure 'requiring every nomination to a curacy to contain one-third of the benefice as the stipend which the curate is to receive'; and in addition that 'every curate of a parish be nominated to his cure, *not* by the incumbent, but by the bishop'. Curates, he went on, suffered at present from an inferiority complex. Incumbents talked of 'my curate' as though he was a servant, assigned to him all the drudgery of parish work, and rarely consulted him or asked his opinion. For instance his vicar might introduce a friend into the pulpit or desk, 'without even asking the assistant-minister whether he was willing to give up his turn'. The public advertisements for curates vividly portrayed their humiliating position : their duties were strictly laid down, even to tutoring their employers' children; they were required willy-nilly to conform to a particular type of churchmanship; they were expected to be at once zealous and humble; and whether or not they would be permitted to engage in secular employments such as schoolmastering depended entirely upon the whim of the incumbent. The author ended his pamphlet with a plea to the bishops to insist upon appointing all curates themselves, whose employment could then only be terminated with their consent; and finally to 'set apart the smaller benefices in their gift for the special use of curates of the Church. These might be preferred in due order, after producing the usual testimonials and after so many years service in the Church'. In this way they would at last extinguish 'all heart-sickening delay of hope on the part of the unbeneficed'. The provision of endowered perpetual curacies, as has been seen, helped to meet this last problem; but it was never really solved. The Exeter diocese, for instance, possessed some sixty-eight curates in 1866 who were earning an average income of £100 per annum and had served at least fifteen and some as many as fifty years in that capacity.

Curates continued to be badly paid despite the Pluralities Act of 1838. Out of twenty-two advertisements for curates in 1858 only two offered £100, while fourteen ranged from £70 to as little as £20. A skilled domestic servant such as a butler, coachman or cook would earn as much as £70 or £80 with all found; and an elementary schoolmaster could expect at least £150 in addition to a rent-free school-house. In the Victorian era incumbents were increasingly associated with their squires and treated with corresponding respect by the laity; but a curate was still fair game for contempt, abuse and even violence. In 1854 a curate was thrown out of a ball-room at Bury because there were objections to his presence; another was foully abused and assaulted by a crowd outside a public house in Bristol when he was on his way to baptise a dying child. *The Habits of Good Society*, which appeared in 1855, differentiated clearly between an incumbent and his assistant when it declared : 'One must never smoke, without consent, in the presence of a clergyman, and one must never offer a cigar to any ecclesiastic over the rank of a curate.'

A memorial signed by eight prominent London assistant curates was submitted to the First Lambeth Conference in 1867, although no time was found to consider it, which made the following points :

That the tenure of an assistant curate is extremely insecure at all times, but especially on the occasion of the vacancy of the benefice; and that this presses most upon those whose curacies are virtually sole charges. That many hardships arise to curates from the fact that the laws relating to the discipline of the clergy in the matter of revocation of licence etc., afford so little protection to those unbeneficed.

That the stipends of curates, who have served some years in the ministry are inadequate, when the uncertainty of their tenure is taken into account. That the present bestowal of patronage, which has little regard to the length of service and merits, generates a restless pursuit of preferment amongst the unbeneficed clergy, by which their energies are distracted from pastoral work, and also from those habits of study which are essential to the effectiveness of a clergyman's ministrations.

That the unbeneficed clergy are not directly represented in the Holy Synods or Convocations, which treat of matters touching the discipline of the Church, and of the clergy thereof.

THE CURATE'S LOT

That owing to the little regard paid to the difference of the offices of the priesthood and the diaconate, assistant curates, who are priests, are oftentimes called upon to discharge the duties properly belonging to the diaconate, to the comparative neglect of that higher work which is the duty and privilege of the priestly office.

The Lambeth Fathers had no time to spare to discuss this appeal; but as the clerical papers continued to be inundated with letters from 'ambitious and disaffected' curates, which were answered by 'alarmed incumbents', it was decided to deal with the whole position of the stipendiary curate at the next Church Congress to be held at Wolverhampton during October 1867. Accordingly on Wednesday, 2 October, two papers were read by the Reverend J. J. Halcombe from Charterhouse and the Reverend G. Osborne Brown from Torquay; after which there was a lively discussion. Various suggestions were put forward by the speakers to relieve grievances and answer 'the poor curate's cry' for a square deal. Mr. Halcombe proposed that 3,000 of the smallest livings should be augmented up to £300 per annum on condition that only curates, who had been engaged in parochial work for at least seven years, were eligible for appointment; that the Church should get rid of 'the dead level system' under which the experienced curate found himself competing on unequal terms with the newly ordained, who were preferred by incumbents simply because they cost less money, by persuading the laity to augment the older man's salary and so take the burden off the shoulders of his employer; and that when curates had to remain in that position for lengthy periods the Additional Curates' Society and the Pastoral Aid Society should 'give materially larger grants towards the income of a curate of five years than to a curate just ordained'. Mr. Osborne Brown in his turn spelt out the many disabilities the curate suffered from in his relations with his incumbent, his bishop and the convocations. There were, for example, 'the derogatory modes of speech and manners of treatment' dealt out to him by his vicar or rector, who thought of him not as a fellow-priest, but as a humble dependent, 'between whom and themselves a great gulf lies'. Then there was the case of the assistant in a large town parish, who has been delegated to a particular sphere of work, 'has carried it on for some time, and is gradually completing it,' when there comes a change of incumbent, and he has to leave, and the work itself is either stopped or referred to others. In such instances, surely, the speaker pleaded, where the bishop has licensed a mission church, the curacy ought to be made a permanency.

He next attacked the autocratic power of the bishop, which at any rate in the case of a resident incumbent was unsupported by law, in refusing or revoking a curate's licence at will, often out of personal prejudice, whereby he and his family were suddenly deprived of their livelihood. A curate, like an incumbent, ought to have the right to a fair trial by law. Instead 'for him there is no regular process of law, no trial by jury; the veriest trifle is accepted against him—a newspaper report, an anonymous letter, may be enough to stop his ministrations; for he is presumed guilty, and mercifully permitted, in certain cases, to show reason to the contrary. He may be separated from the people who respect him, from the incumbent who values him, and at a moments' warning be deprived of the means of earning his daily bread. Well may the ranks of the clergy be thinning.' For Mr. Osborne Brown believed that this was one of the principal reasons for men not taking Holy Orders.

Out of nearly 13,000 livings only about 3,000 were in the gift of the bishops and incumbents of mother churches, and so open to the ordinary run-of-the-mill curate; and here, all too often, men were brought in from outside the diocese and promoted over the heads of deserving local assistants. The solution lay in admitting to livings only men who had served seven years in holy orders, in confining the bishops' patronage to curates who had served a term of seven years in the same diocese, and in compelling patrons to sell their advowsons only to the Church, when the patronage would be vested not only in bishop and archdeacon, but in the churchwardens and two lay communicants of the parishes concerned. All this would encourage the unknown curate, who did not truckle for favours, to hope for a settled home, where he could bring up his family without having to suffer the continual expense and inconvenience of moving from one curacy to another.

Finally assistant curates, large numbers of whom were men of maturity, experience and learning, should have the right to vote for proctors in convocation and even to stand for election to a seat in that august body; since it was not the freehold but the priesthood that ought to constitute the proper qualification.

In the discussion that followed the reading of these two papers several curates took a prominent part. The Reverend Walter Blunt advocated that no one be allowed to become an incumbent under thirty years of age, because 'an old curate can seldom work satisfactorily under a young incumbent. He is the superior of his superior. He has had too much experience, and knows too much; and is continually treading on his incumbent's toes without intending it.' He himself was still a curate at fifty years of age, and had worked in parishes large and small throughout the country; yet 'I believe during my whole curate life my average income was about £90 a year'. The Reverend R. I. Salmon, curate of St. Michael's, Paddington, refused to believe that there were now any curates who 'did not enjoy equality of priesthood—which means equality of rights in the parish—with his incumbent'; but he was seriously concerned about their stipends and what he termed 'the iniquitous patronage system': 'There is nothing that more provokes—I might say disgusts—a man, than seeing one whom he knows to be his inferior, both morally and intellectually, who has been marked tekel over and over again in his University career, nevertheless as soon as he has been twelve months in Orders, put into a comfortable rectory.' It is particularly infuriating when he himself has worked hard as a curate for ten or fifteen years without any improvement either in his stipend or his chances of preferment.

Contrariwise the curate himself came in for some criticism,

and the 'poor curates' cry' deprecated. Archdeacon Allen (Salop) commented on the easy priesting of deacons : 'A curate goes to a parish as a deacon. Perhaps he gives his mind to croquet parties and preaches sermons which he transcribes from the first book he takes down from his shelf. The farmers see what an empty negligent fellow he is, but they say, "when he goes up for ordination my Lord Bishop will find him out" . . . But the Bishop says it is a pity to send this young man back to his parish disgraced.' No man, the Archdeacon went on to argue, ought to be priested until he is quite fit for that high office.

The Reverend C. Deane discounted the whole agitation and amid cheers roundly declared that curates had little or nothing to complain about :

In the first place there is no body of men who have gained more in position during the last five-and-twenty years than the curates have done. By their living and their labour they have gained for themselves an independent position which is improving daily. Their services are daily more and more sought after, and their stipends have increased. Let them go on and their work will be valued more and more. As for what has been said about the tyranny of incumbents and the unkindness of incumbents' wives, that is all nonsense. . . . As to what has been said about the equality of curates in point of consideration and remuneration I deny it in toto. Curates of a certain standing who have shown themselves fit for their work, may not only demand and receive greater respect, but may also demand and receive a higher remuneration for their services than curates of a single year. . . . I know an instance of a man coming into a parish with a stipend gradually rising to £100. . . . Nor is this a solitary instance. . . . If our stipends were largely increased the effect would be that we should get not a higher but a lower class of men for Holy Orders . . . at present . . . candidates for Holy Orders are for the most part actuated by disinterested motives.

However, there was one thing at least about which he was deeply concerned : pensions for aged clergymen whether curates or incumbents. 'It is the duty of the State to provide pensions for the clergy who have become incapacitated and grown old in the service of the State as well as the Church.' The discussion ended on this note, after it had been disclosed that the bishops of Oxford and Lichfield at any rate bestowed all the patronage at their disposal upon curates in their respective dioceses. The Congress passed on to other subjects, the agitation died down, and curates continued much as before. But the fact that they were held in little esteem was sometimes merited by their conduct. The Reverend B. J. Armstrong, the loquacious high church vicar of East Dereham, Norfolk, wrote in his diary concerning the curate of Cawston, whom he found presiding over a school feast in the absence of the rector, that he 'was clad in check trousers, buff waistcoat, and holland blouse, no neckerchief and a nautical cap. I never saw anyone so unlike a clergyman in all respects. Such a person must be quite ignorant of the dignity and solemnity attaching to his office.' Armstrong also said of one of his own curates in September 1863 : 'My curate leaves me tomorrow and I shall be alone. His reason for going is that he cannot live, he says, on £100 a year. I have never felt safe with him, and his ministrations are worth little. He may not be able to live on £100 a year, but he is not *worth* that as a matter of value.'

Harvey Bloom, who was ordained 24 February 1888 and went to Hertford for his first curacy under Canon Clive Wigram, also received £100 per annum and did not get on with his employer. But he was well worth the money since he carried out all the slogging work in the parish, ran numerous clubs and visited assiduously. The canon, however, 'looked down his nose' and poured could water on his curate's endeavours. It is true that Harvey, who was big, robust and impulsive, sometimes let his enthusiasms out-run his discretion. On one occasion, returning from a football match clad in navy blue shorts and a too small vest, he was informed that a lady parishioner was seriously ill. Not waiting to change he rushed to her bedside; but, alas, as she afterwards complained to the vicar, there was a gap between shorts and vest that disclosed his navel. The canon was horrified and informed his curate : 'It is never to occur again.' 'Just the sort of thing to that would happen to me,' Harvey commented

142

in his diary, 'it all comes of being too fat.' After six months he could stand it no longer; and finding plenty of vacancies for curates advertised in *The Church Times*, he secured one at Harwich under a Mr. Druce, who was prepared to pay him £120 per annum and leave him to his own devices. 'Mr. Druce told stories of previous curates who had driven him mad; the fat and dumpling one who thought of nothing but his food, and did practically nothing; the lean one who drank on the sly, and had to leave because once he preached when intoxicated; the friend's son who had got the maid into trouble, and in the end had bolted with a valued parishioner's wife.' 'But,' he concluded hopefully, 'you will be different.' Harvey, who was now married and lived in a large house for the very reasonable rent of £18 a year, was certainly very different. He stayed for two years and worked like a black for his half-starved parishioners : 'He would walk ten miles to get them a hospital ticket. . . . It was Harvey who did a house to house tour at Christmas begging oranges for the children; Harvey who got up a collection for Christmas comforts for the old people.' From Harwich he moved to the mining village of Hemsworth, Yorkshire, and then to the country parish of Springfield near Chelmsford. So in a few years he had moved four times. His chief failing was an over-fondness for young ladies, whom he used to take for botanical expeditions at Harwich and on the river at Springfield. Eventually he got involved with a Sunday school teacher, gave up parish work and went as headmaster to a small school in Long Marston, Warwickshire.

The story of William Henry Whitworth, 1834 to 1885, is even more typical of the average curate's odyssey. A Fellow of Corpus Christi College, Oxford, and ordained in 1834 by Bishop Bagot as deacon, and priested the following year, he resigned his Fellowship in 1836 in order to marry and become a schoolmaster, first at Kensington and later at Dedham Free Grammar School, where he also did some duty in the parish church. In 1847 he was headmaster of Totnes Grammar School, earning a salary of £150 a year. The school declined and Whitworth finally abandoned teaching for parish work in 1848, when he became assistant curate of St. Thomas', Dudley. But urban life did not suit his growing family, and an epidemic of cholera sent him flying into the country to become curate to Stephen Hawtrey, vicar of Alvedison, Broadchalke and Bowerchalke, Wiltshire, who was non-resident, an invalid, and apparently uninterested in his parishes, which he left to the care of his two curates. However, he was not prepared to support Whitworth when the latter quarrelled with some influential parishioners, but compelled him to resign. Whitworth then moved to Great Doddington, Northamptonshire, under the headmaster of Wellingborough Grammar School, Thomas Sanderson, a 'fierce and bearded Doctor of Divinity', who 'had a reputation for using his curates as schoolmasters'. He next applied to James Boys, vicar of Biddenden, Kent, for a title, enclosing a glowing testimonial from Sanderson, who described him as 'a sound and orthodox churchman' and 'a scholar and gentleman, well calculated to influence people with Mrs. Whitworth, a valuable assistant both in the schools and societies connected with the Church'. But unfortunately Hawtrey, when consulted by Archbishop Sumner, voiced a very different opinion: 'For some time before Mr. Whitworth quitted my curacy,' he wrote, 'very unfavourable reports had reached me as to the details of his character when the parties on my preferring to write to the bishop would not allow me to use their names: I was only relieved from this perplexing state of things by Mr. Whitworth's resignation.' Sumner promptly passed this letter on to Mr. Boys, who replied: 'I am most grieved to receive yr Grace's intimations respecting Mr. Whitworth which will at once put an end to the engagement.' A decision scarcely fair to his new curate, since he had also been informed on unimpeachable authority 'that Mr. Hawtrey was not only non-resident but not in a fit state to take interest in his parish', which Whitworth had served faithfully for four years 'without having seen his vicar who could not give him a testimonial of personal knowledge'. But Boys was taking no chances, and obviously in deference to the archbishop's wishes threw Whitworth to the wolves, who was compelled to take a series of uncongenial curacies, first at St. Mary's, Beighton, near Sheffield and then at Llanbedr in Breconshire, from the last of which he had to retire almost at once since he could speak no Welsh. None the less his vicar, Edward Lewis, sent him on to his next incumbent, Sir William Palmer, vicar of Whitchurch Canonicorum, near Bridport, with the following handsome testimonial: 'During the period that Mr. Whitworth has been with me I can speak of him in the highest terms from his attention to my school and church duties. I deeply regret being deprived of so valuable a kind friend.' Whitworth, then, had moved nine times in twenty-three years, being always prepared to adapt his churchmanship to his company. Boys, for example, was a strict evangelical, while his last vicar, William Palmer, was a pronounced Tractarian and liturgiologist. He was now put in sole charge of Chideock, which only brought him in the small stipend of £80, and stayed there for the next seventeen years in indigent circumstances. They could never afford more than one servant, so that Mrs. Whitworth wore herself to the bone and died from tuberculosis in 1876. At last William, now sixty-six years of age, was offered his first and last living at Ratlinghoe, near Shrewsbury, which boasted a population of 300 souls and a stipend of no more than £60 per annum. Here he married again, had yet another child in 1881, and died some four years later, leaving, one is surprised to learn, an estate worth £2,051 2s. 5d., which may well have come to him through his second marriage.

In a curious little pamphlet entitled *My Rectors by a Quondam Curate*, published in 1890, the relationship between employer and employed is amusingly set forth. The curate begins by confessing that his own preparation for the ministry was far from adequate. He took a degree in mathematics at Cambridge, but studied little else. 'My Theology!' he wrote, 'I blush when I think of it. It consisted in little more than could be squeezed out of a boiled-down Paley, and the dry notes on the one Gospel in Greek Testament required for the Littlego.' On the strength of this and a glowing testimonial from his college dons, none of whom he had ever spoken to outside a lecture hall, he was ordained deacon to a title which he had obtained as the result of an advertisement. His first rector was a country gentleman, who treated him very well and left him to his own devices; the squire invited him to dinner and half promised him a living in his gift. Then came disaster. One of the squire's labourers had listened to a socialist agitator speaking on the village green, where-upon he was given the sack and evicted from his cottage. The curate courageously remonstrated with the squire, who reported him to the rector, and on his refusing to apologise he was com-pelled to hand in his resignation. His second rector was a learned and wealthy high churchman, who kept his curate in his place and his nose to the grindstone. 'Mr. Lordling generally preached both morning and evening. But he believed in division of labour. He re-quired his Curate to teach in the Sunday School, to address the old women in the afternoon, and to take the cottage lectures on winter week-nights.' When, however, on rare occasions the curate did preach, Mr. Lordling subjected his sermons to merciless and public criticism. For instance 'in preaching a funeral sermon one Sunday evening I quoted the text, "O death, where is thy sting? O grave, where is thy victory?" laying a slight emphasis on the *where*. The following Sunday, Mr. Lordling dragged the same text into his sermon in so marked a manner that most of the congregation recognised he did it for the Curate's benefit. His reading was "O death, where IS thy sting, O grave where IS thy victory".' But the unforgivable sin was when some of the parishioners asked the rector if the curate might preach more frequently. 'The request,' commented the latter, 'led to his neither preaching nor reading, but departing.' His third rector was a fashionable London incumbent, who expected his curate to do all the work, while he took all the credit. As long as this arrange-ment was adhered to all was well. 'The division of labour at S. Silas' was this—the Rector preached one sermon a week, the Curate did all the rest of the parish work.' Mr. Tufter's late curate, Mr. Brown, had fulfilled these conditions to the letter: 'Who established the District Visitors' Guild? Mr. Brown the last curate. Who started the Working Men's Club? Mr. Brown the last curate. Who visited the sick and poor? Who catechised the children and kept the Sunday School in such perfect discipline? Who, in fine, was the life and soul of the parish? Why, Mr. Brown, the last curate. On my asking a poor old woman whom I visited, if the Rector did not come to see her, she replied, "Why, bless your heart, Sir, not one of the neighbours never sees he. He be too grand for we. Mr. Brown was our man".' Mr. Tufter preached in the morning to a fashionable congregation, and the curate in the evening, when the few well-to-do ladies present made a point of leaving the church immediately before the sermon with a great rustling of silk dresses, 'to impress the rest of the congregation that to be in time for dinner was far more important than listening to a curate's sermon.' Furthermore it quickly became apparent that his addresses were of a dangerous character. Mr. Tufter was compelled to take him aside after one such discourse and to comment that 'such opinions as I had expressed tended to make people dissatisfied with their lot in life—they were apt to cause a not sufficient recognition of class distinctions'. This, of course, was equivalent to a notice to quit, and our 'Quondam curate' was soon on his travels again.

A sequel appeared in the same year, *My Curates by a Rector*, that put the opposite point of view. The rector indeed began by asserting 'that many curates are by no means anxious to exchange their status for that of incumbent of a small living. The curate is, in many respects, the more independent; he has few calls on his purse, while the incumbent has many; and the sense of parochial responsibility falls much more heavily on the incumbent than on a curate. Besides this, I am aware that not a few young men in Holy Orders have refused livings on principle, deeming it their duty to remain Curates for a term of at least ten years.' He then went on to define his own position towards his curates: 'We have always wished to treat our curates as our equals and on terms of intimacy. They have been expected to come, as a matter of course, to dinner and supper on Sunday, and could drop in at any time and be welcomed. . . . I have been ready to receive from them any suggestions which might be serviceable to the spiritual welfare of the parish. If I found fault with them there is little doubt that they had reason to find fault with me.'

None the less despite this liberal policy, he appears to have suffered considerably at the hands of some of his assistants. At one time he was rector of the important parish of St. Peter, Mulworth, which required the services of an able preacher. This was supplied in the person of an experienced forty-year-old evangelical curate, the Reverend Sampson Slimmer, whose flamboyant, extempore discourses immediately put those of his employer in the shade. 'My curate,' the latter ruefully remarked, 'was a huge cannon; I but a pop-gun.' The congregation got into the habit of slipping away after the third collect when they knew the rector was preaching, but filled the church to over-flowing in order to hear the curate. Neither was this the worst. Mr. Slimmer started a prayer-meeting at which he used to petition the Almighty in a fervent voice 'for his dear fellow-labourer' and 'for the weak Shepherd at the head of the parish'. Eventually the congregation became so large that it was decided to build a new church and subdivide the parish. Mr. Slimmer became its first vicar and married the maiden lady who had subscribed most of the money for its erection.

The rector's next curate, the Reverend Roger Rashleigh, was a Cambridge cricket blue, dressed like a layman, and voiced the most disturbing socialist views. He spoke of Queen Victoria as 'a decent old lady, utterly unnecessary to the Welfare of the State', and referred to the House of Lords as 'a stop-gap to enlightenment and progress'. When reminded by his employer of the teaching of the Catechism, he replied: 'he had yet to learn whether the Lords were his betters, and as to the Catechism, why it was a relic of serfdom, and compiled by some Erastian sycophant of the Reformation'. But worse still he took it upon himself to instruct the rector's wife as to how she should play her game of whist, called the local Tory M.P., Sir Thomas Scratcham, 'Sir Bombastes Nincompoop', and sneered at Lady Scratcham as 'a Yorkshire breweress'. The rector then was not altogether sorry when a well-connected relative offered Mr. Rashleigh a country living. However, his third curate, the Reverend Marmaduke Maypole, was even more trying. He was a high churchman, who took advantage of his employer's absence in America for six months on a visit to his son, to change the whole ethos of the parish church. So on his return the rector found that 'Mr. Maypole had adopted coloured stoles . . . the choir was now in cassocks as well as surplices; a processional hymn was sung before the service; and at the head of the procession Captain Filbert marched with a cross in his hands. . . . A very uncivil war had also been declared in the columns of *The Mulworth Weekly Express*! Letters signed by "Churchman" and "a Protestant" succeeded each other; they were more rude than logical.' Weakly he accepted the situation and 'submitted to be vested in a short, tight-fitting surplice and coloured stole'. Mr. Maypole, the son of a yeoman, also felt that advanced churchmanship merited a distinguished birth: 'His paper and envelopes were ordained with a crest, a hand holding a pole, with the motto "Excelsior" underneath. I was informed that Baron Maypole fought at the battle of Crecy.' Unlike Mr. Rashleigh he met the Scratchams hat in hand when they came to church and held the carriage door open for them to alight. He visited Scratcham Court regularly, and invariably arrived just before luncheon. Posing at first as a celibate, he quickly succumbed to the principle of 'don't marry for money, but go where the money is', courted and wedded the niece of a wealthy brewer, and with her money purchased himself a rich advowson to which he presented himself.

His successor, the Reverend Peter Parchment, was an even higher churchman, who in a quiet, civil, dreamy way drifted over into Rome on the assumption, or so his rector strongly suspected, that 'Manning and Newman went over to Rome; they were great men. Therefore, if I go over to Rome I must be a great man'.

A final curate, the Reverend Ernest Verity, was a very different type. He was a great admirer of the authors of *Essays and Reviews* and soaked himself in the higher criticism of the Bible. At a deanery chapter meeting he read a paper on Biblical Inspiration that shocked his more conservative brethren; and when the rural dean denounced him as a second Colenso he had the temerity to answer back. Subsequently he decided not to proceed to the priesthood, but to send in his resignation instead, which was thankfully accepted. Such were the main characters in the pamphlet; but the rector also mentions a Mr. Sayce, who always agreed with him on the principle that 'my views are those of my Rector'; and a Mr. Valentine Spooney, who courted two girls in the parish at the same time, which, when it was discovered by their enraged fathers, necessitated the curate taking the first available train to London. There was also the story of a temporary curate, Ferdinand Lefanue, a Canadian clergyman on holiday with excellent references, whom the rector engaged for three months and paid in advance. A charming and cultivated man, he persuaded a number of wealthy parishioners to contribute substantial sums towards a mission in Canada; and then left unobtrusively at the end of the first month. 'His sudden departure was owing to his fear of the police; he was not a clergyman, but a ticket of leave man.'

In conclusion, somewhat wistfully, the rector outlined the qualities that he would like to see in the ideal curate. Preferably a graduate of Oxford or Cambridge, he must have his heart in his work, but not strive after a cheap popularity. The friend of the rich as well as of the poor, he should be cheerful, contented and loyal to his rector, while free from affectation, mannerisms and servility. Above all he ought to be in possession of the three cardinal virtues of humility, zeal and a determination to do his duty without thought of preferment :

150

Charge once more, then, and be dumb
Let the Victors when they come,
When the forts of folly fall
Find thy body by the wall.

The well-to-do curate had of course a very different row to hoe
from that of his poor brother. Francis Goddard, a member of an
old Welsh family, whose father was vicar and lord of the manor
at Clyffe Pypard in Wiltshire, has described in *Reminiscences of
a Wiltshire Vicar, 1814–1893,* his experiences as a curate, first at
Winterbourne Bassett from 1837 to 1842; then, after a two years'
holiday abroad, he passed in swift succession through three more
curacies: Matherne near Chepstow, Writhlington near Rad-
stock in Somerset, and Cameley also in Somerset, before being
appointed to the living of Alderton in Wiltshire in 1849. His
salary ranged from £80 to £130, but he had private means and
usually lived in the parsonage of his non-resident rector, employing two maid-servants and a gardener-groom. He hunted at
Winterbourne Bassett and indulged in other sports such as archery
and cricket, dined with the squire and was generally regarded
by the fashionable members of his congregation as a friend and a
social equal. He worked hard, took two Sunday services, visited
the sick and helped the poor. At Writhlington he built a school.
Curates then had a reputation for drinking heavily, and when he
dined with his rector as Cameley, the latter invariably watered
the wine! They were also supposed to preach very long sermons.
Goddard tells the following story of a neighbouring curate at
Grittleton, Edward Awdry. 'I went at 11 a.m. to do duty at
Stanton St. Quintin, I could hear Awdry preaching as I went
past Grittleton church; I came back at half-past three p.m. and he
was still going on.' Let us hope it was to a different congregation! He comments sadly on the condition of some of his less
fortunate brethren : 'Mr. Walsh was one of those wasted intellects
one sometimes meets with—a double-first class, many years curate
at Tockenham at £80 per annum. . . . Luckington is very near
Alderton and here dwelt one Thomas Teasdale, curate for a

good many years, breeding up a family of five children on £80 per annum. He was a very learned man, a great Greek scholar, engaged in making a lexicon for ten years, when Liddell and Scott published their Lexicon and forever destroyed poor Teasdale's chance of any benefit from his long years of literary toil. After the death of his rector, Mr. Birch, of Easton Grey, Mr. Teasdale removed to Hullavington, where he gradually in extreme penury wasted away. His two sons, who were simply labourers, emigrated to Australia with one of the daughters. One daughter became insane amidst their manifold privations, and the remaining one, May Teasdale, became a needle woman in the firm of Jones and Co. of Bristol, where I heard of her as by degrees starving upon wages of 6s. per week.'

Clive Archer, the son of a Herefordshire land-owner, who was educated at Harrow and Oxford, spent the time waiting for the family living of Solihull to fall vacant by touring the Continent and living at home where he did occasional duty in neighbouring churches. But despite this carefree existence he was far from happy. 'I remember,' he wrote in his diary, 'being in want of a separate home and being dissatisfied with my position as living at home without any independence; yet without reason, for my allowance, three hundred, was ample and my father very kind. But the house and its ways was not agreeable for a young clergyman, and I suppose that most men at that age want to be masters somewhere, so I was very glad when I got leave and opportunity to go abroad again.' In 1829 the incumbent of Solihull died and Clive immediately succeeded to the living. His feelings and those of his family upon hearing the news of his good fortune are vividly described in the diary: 'In January 1829 I and my brother George and my father were sitting after dinner in the library at Whitfield when the post arrived. My father took and opened the newspaper and after reading for some time exclaimed, "By Jove. Old Curtis is dead". A letter which had come by the same post from his son confirmed the intelligence. I perfectly well remember my feelings on the occasion. They were certainly not of sorrow for I had never seen the deceased and I was heartily tired of the objectless life which I had led while living at my father's. But assuredly my feelings were not all joy. I cannot describe them. A sensation of great change, a feeling that I had a home distinct from the paternal one, and also a feeling of the great charge I was to undertake of a large parish among strangers and I totally inexperienced in everything like business whether professional or otherwise. My father felt only joy at my having come into what he then believed to be two thousand a year, but his congratulations grated in some degree on my ear and were not in accordance with the mixed feelings I have attempted to describe, and I took an early opportunity of going to my own room where I knelt down and prayed and resolved to do my best as a parish priest.'

Unlike Clive Archer, who spoke so bitterly of his 'objectless life' at home and desired so passionately an independency of his own, John Keble, the famous Tractarian, was prepared to sacrifice his career again and again in order to help his father, the vicar of Coln St. Aldwyn near Fairford in Gloucestershire. In 1823 he resigned his Oriel Fellowship to take the curacy of Southrop, a few miles from his home, so that he could be at hand when needed; and later in 1826 left the curacy of Hursley in Hampshire, where he had spent a happy year 'of clear shining', to return once again to his aged parent's side, now a widower and also bereaved of a beloved daughter, Mary Anne, to shoulder the task of his curate at Coln St. Aldwyn. Here John remained, deaf to many tempting offers and in the clear knowledge that in the eyes of his contemporaries he was regarded as a 'near-failure', until at last old Mr. Keble's death in 1834 set him free to marry and to return to his beloved Hursley as its vicar.

Another well-born curate was the Hon. Edward Bligh, whose marriage to Lady Isabel Nevill, daughter of the earl of Abergavenny, himself a clergyman, was made conditional by her father on the bridegroom, who was the son of the earl of Darnley, giving up the diplomatic service for that of the Church. 'Young

Bligh,' he said, 'wanted his daughter. He could have her provided he anchored himself to his native country by dropping the diplomatic service. A surer and holier substitute could be provided. His Lordship had no less than twenty-four livings in his gift, some of them uncommonly fat ones. Let the young man enter the Church, and a suitable living could be guaranteed in a short time. That was the offer, and he could take it or leave it.' Bligh liked it; but before he could accept any living he had first to take a university degree, then a *sine qua non*, and secure the title to a curacy. The latter, as he frankly admitted, was 'no bone fide title at all', since the vicar of Cobham, the Darnleys' family home, provided him one 'pro forma', on the strength of which he was ordained in 1855. However, soon afterwards he went as a genuine curate to Snodland, an industrial parish of some four thousand inhabitants, mostly cement and lime workers, whose rector, the Reverend W. Phelps, was over eighty years of age. Bligh and his wife lived 'in a tiny habitation near the Bull Inn', where he played at being a curate, and received an unwanted salary of £80, which their eccentric old rector brought to them personally every quarter. 'On quarter day,' wrote Bligh in his journal, 'when my stipend of £25 was due, the old gentleman would triumphantly march up the village to our house and put the money down in hard cash.' Otherwise he was left very much to his own devices, except that he was warned on arrival to keep his sermons short. 'Twelve minutes,' he was told, 'is long enough for any *monkey* to be talking to a lot of others.' Then after a year, when he had been priested, he was presented by his father-in-law to the benefice of Rotherfield in Sussex.

To 'top off' this list of well-to-do curates there is the story of the Reverend Octavius Pickard-Cambridge, who was ordained in 1858 by the bishop of Chester and licensed to the curacy of Scarisbrick, then part of the parish of Ormskirk, whose incumbent, Joseph Bush, paid him a stipend of £60 per annum. But since the squire of Scarisbrick was a Roman Catholic, who would not allow a clergyman of the Church of England to live on his estate, Pickard-Cambridge was compelled to lodge in Southport and walk the considerable distance to his church. None the less he found plenty of time to carry on his hobby of natural history, and in 1860 published a list of the Southport spiders in *The Zoologist*. In that year he resigned Scarisbrick and became his father's curate at Bloxworth in Dorset, where he lived in a cottage belonging to the rectory. The light duties of the two tiny parishes of Bloxworth and Winterbourne-Tomson left him ample leisure both to continue his collection of spiders and to travel extensively both in the British Isles and on the Continent. In 1865 he 'visited every part of the Holy Land and went as far north as Damascus'. A permanent memorial of this last expedition is to be found in the east window of Bloxworth church, where the representation of Our Lord's empty tomb is based on a sketch he made of a tomb near Jerusalem. The next year he married Rose Wallace, and in 1868 succeeded his father and moved into Bloxworth rectory. His apprenticeship was now over and he settled down happily to the life of a country squarson.

The Reverend E. B. Ellman was not quite in this category; but his father had purchased for him the advowson of Berwick in Sussex during 1837, and when the son came down from Oxford a year later with a first-class degree he went straight to Berwick as curate to the rector, Mr. Henry West. West himself never visited his parish, but spent his forty-nine years' incumbency at Lewes. Ellman, who lived in the rectory with one general servant, received £40 a year only, for which he was expected to prepare and preach two sermons a Sunday. But as he was only a deacon he had to find outside help for a celebration, for which he must pay out of his own pocket. He could not afford to do this and so there was no communion service at Christmas, and at Easter only on Low Sunday, when he was able to exchange with a neighbouring incumbent. 'I had learned,' he wrote in his *Recollections*, 'to be very economical. I kept pigs and worked very hard in my garden in my leisure hours, sending what I grew to the market at Lewes. I had started a Dame's school in a cottage, and Clothing and Coal Clubs, and all required money, which I had to supply myself. It was seldom that I had any butcher's meat, and my suit of clerical clothes lasted me four years before I could buy more. . . . Newspapers and books were luxuries I could not afford.' Fifteen months after his arrival he was priested; but conditions were little easier. The rector, who had agreed to furnish the rectory and pay its rates, supplied only the barest minimum of the former and tried to get out of doing the latter altogether. Furthermore 'he made several attempts to lower the £40 a year I received'. Ellman remained for six and a half years as curate of Berwick, being absent from the parish for only one night; but in 1844 he left to become vicar of Wartling, when his successor, Mr. Pruen, found his employer equally awkward. 'When he came over to see the house,' wrote Ellman, 'he complained of the scanty furniture. I explained that some of it was my own, and that the stove in the hall belonged to me. . . . Mr. Pruen went to Mr. West and said he could not take the curacy unless he too had a stove and some more furniture.' In the end the rector purchased Ellman's stove, having failed to persuade him to leave it behind him, free, gratis and for nothing. 'However much I had neglected my parish,' the latter commented bitterly, 'my rector would neither have known nor cared.'

Not all incumbents, of course, treated their curates like this. John Armstrong, who was curate of Dinder, Somerset, from 1835 to 1845 under Dr. Jenkyns, master of Balliol, was treated almost like a son. He had been an undergraduate under Jenkyns, who 'afforded him a decisive proof of the high opinion which was entertained of his merits by offering him a title for Holy Orders through a nomination to the curacy of his own parish of Dinder'. While the master was at Oxford Armstrong lived in the rectory that Jenkyns had built; but when he arrived for the Easter and summer vacations, the curate, his wife and growing family were packed off for an extended holiday in Cornwall. According to a memoir of him written by his wife, Armstrong worked hard and was greatly beloved in the village, of which through the influence of Jenkyns, now Dean of Wells, he became rector in 1845. Moreover the dean gave some land adjoining the rectory, which he had bought out of his own pocket, to be laid out as a garden in 1850. He also assisted in greatly enlarging the house in order to accommodate the Armstrong family. So his assistant 'changed the place of curate for that of incumbent and was thus entrusted with the sole superintendence of the little flock to which he had already endeared himself by a loving devotion'. He died at Dinder in 1862 at the age of fifty-one.

Richard Wilton, the poet, was equally well-treated. After leaving Cambridge in 1851 he became curate to the Reverend and Hon. Orlando Forester, rector of Broseley in Shropshire, and tutor to his small son, Cecil. Here he lived in the rectory and was at first most happy and comfortable. He wrote to his brother Edward:

He offered me the curacy of Linley. He intends to establish a weekly service there which I would take. Indeed I should be in sole charge of the place. My only other Sunday duty would be to read prayers at Broseley in the mornings. My salary would be £60 (a year) and my time would be my own after six o'clock in the evening. Besides this, a nephew of (a neighbour) Miss Stables is coming to be under my tuition along with Cecil which will be a great relief out of school hours and no additional trouble in teaching. He is eight years old, and I think a little emulation and contradiction would do Cecil good. His father would pay me for his education. Now I think this is as gentle and easy an introduction to the ministerial life as I am likely to have. I should be able to hear sermons and have time to study, besides the comfort of a home. And I do feel at home. I love Mr. Forester more and more. No one could be more uniformly kind to me. Mrs. Forester is very kind too, and they have made my room so comfortable and all my wants are so amply supplied that as far as the body is concerned I have nothing to wish for. Tuition is hard work, but when my duties cease at six will not be so irksome. Cecil gets on well with his studies. I have gained control over him as well as his affection.

But he quickly found that a curacy was not entirely a bed of roses. Cecil became unmanageable. 'As far as Cecil is concerned,' he wrote, 'my life here is bitterness. He is so disobedient and void of feeling and so utterly intractable that I earnestly long to have done with him.' Mrs. Mortimer, the great lady of the village, complained of his preaching voice, and he had to present himself at the Hall for instruction. His parents, who were in financial difficulties, demanded and received the greater part of his salary; and finally a young lady, whom he had fallen in love with, was monopolised by a fellow curate, Mr. Hazeldine, who 'so devoured her with his eyes that there was nothing left for me'. Wilton therefore determined to go as a missionary to China, a project which he was only prevented from undertaking by a poor constitution. Instead he moved to another curacy.

Another evangelical, William Andrew, who was curate successively of Gimingham and Witchingham in Norfolk before his appointment to the living of Ketteringham in 1845, was equally hard-working and well-beloved, but his treatment at the hands of the rector of Gimingham was very different. The latter suddenly decided to reside and the curate was dismissed at a moment's notice, just when his wife was expecting her first child. They had nowhere to go, and were already packing to leave before their friends found them the curacy at Witchingham, where the vicar, Dr. Jeans, was also a non-resident. But Andrew was only here a year before Dr. Jeans died, and once again it looked as though he would be cast upon the world to sink or swim; then out of the blue came the presentation to Ketteringham. When he first went to Witchingham he met with a hostile reception because of his evangelical views. The previous curate, Mr. Reynolds, refused to allow his furniture into the house, and he could not get any repairs done. But his earnest labours quickly won his parishioners' hearts, and when he left there were some affecting scenes. At his farewell service 'he was obliged to have the surplice handed over the heads of the congregation from the communion table. As they walked down the aisle Mrs. Howard, who a few months before had bounced out of church in a rage, pressed through the throng and seized Ellen's hand, silently weeping. From the church the people formed a path between two lines, and the Andrews hurried through them, handkerchiefs pressed to their eyes. The crowds followed them across the fields.'

The nineteenth century is particularly rich in unpublished clerical diaries, some of which give us a good picture of the curate at work in his parish. One such diarist was Richard Seymour, who sprang from a famous West Country naval family, and served curacies in the early 'thirties at Havant, Blunham and All Souls, Langham Place, before being collated to his first and only parish of Kinwarton with Great Alne and Wheatley in Warwickshire on 29 May 1835. In these early days Seymour was a strong evangelical although his churchmanship was to change later on; and when the diary opens on 1 January 1832 we find him installed at Havant, acting as assistant curate to a sick friend, Robert Mountain, and also doing duty at Blendworth and Idsworth. He was then a very serious-minded not to say priggish bachelor of twenty-six, much addicted to the study of 'good books', shunning all frivolous amusements like dancing and card-playing, virtuously condemning the luxury and idleness of the rich, and firmly convinced of his own coming premature demise. 'For several nights passed I have been frequently awakened by the pain in my heart which seems to be increasing. If it excites in me apprehensions may this be directed to the important purpose of making me more watchful over myself and more earnest in prayer to God that I may be thus thro' my Redeemer's merits found ready, whensoever it shall please Him to call me hence.' Actually this was no more than a *malade imaginaire* and was finally disposed of by the doctor who examined him at the time of his marriage some three years later. It never prevented him however from working extremely hard, visiting the sick constantly, teaching in the school, and lecturing at the Poor House.

February 16, 1832. While in the work house this evening the thought struck me, how different this scene from that of last night [when there had been a ball at his father's house near Portsmouth]. *There* the handsome, well furnished and well-lighted room. Here a cheerless, comfortless space with one small candle to throw light on my book. *There* Youth and Beauty and affluence and careless hearts. Here the maimed, the blind, the halt, the aged, the sick, the deprived of reason, all, too, poor and destitute but for the aid of others. *There* the sound of music and revelry, mixed with the happy laughs. Here, the crying infant or the moan of the more aged. Most different indeed! His blessing upon my ministry that these may become poor in spirit as they are poor in this world's goods, and that their heavenly and eternal prospects may grow brighter and clearer as their earthly hopes wax more dim and dismal.

He added piously that he hoped and prayed that the riches and pleasures of this life would not prevent his own relations and friends from reaching heaven. He was particularly conscientious in his sermon composition :

February 10. Returned to Havant. Read more of *Henry Martyn.* Would that I had more of his zeal and of the grace which was bestowed upon him. Wasted three hours in making a laboured commencement to my sermon and then went to bed in despair. I fear there is much *pride*, much desire of *the praise of men* at the bottom of this. May the Lord pardon me and humble me, if it shall be His will, and take from me this proud spirit and make His glory the end and aim of all my actions. . . . February 11. Employed all day in writing a sermon and only finished at 2 a.m. on Sunday morning.

He was equally zealous in his visiting that occupied a great deal of time :

June 30. Sent for to see Mrs. Hoare : in a dying state. . . . July 1. Went to administer the sacrament to Mrs. Hoare. Too ill to receive it. Apparently on the eve of quitting this world. Prayed with her. Much affected. Only 29! fear her children in all probability now motherless! Her soul has perhaps already left its earthly tabernacle and is now in the presence of God . . . may the merits of her Saviour have been imparted to her. July 2. Heard Mrs. Hoare was dead.

He took great pains over his confirmation candidates at a time when this type of instruction was very much in its infancy.

May 27. Made arrangements for seeing the candidates for confirmation. . . . June 14. Candidates for Confirmation lamentably ignorant. . . . July 29. Examined for the last time the male candi-

dates for confirmation. Much lamentable ignorance. Many scruples
about admitting them. But their ignorance not their own fault, and
if much knowledge is necessary know not when they are to acquire
it . . . saw female candidates for the last time. May the Lord bless
the laying on of his servant's hands to the increase of their spiritual
strength and their growth in every christian grace for Jesus' sake.
Amen.

When Robert Mountain recovered his health Seymour quitted
Havant in August 1832 and took charge of his elder brother John's
parish of Northchurch in Hertfordshire, while the latter went on
holiday. Here in September there was a sharp out-break of cholera,
and the diarist nobly stood by his people. He assiduously visited
and prayed with the sick, buried the dead and preached to and
taught the healthy. He described the symptoms as 'vomiting,
freezing and cramps'. At the same time he was compelled to take
in pupils in order to supplement his income, and promised a
certain Mr. Drake, 'to instruct his two sons for three hours every
day'. He added the comment: 'a tax on my time, but poverty
demands it, and I must be more industrious at other seasons'.
In November he accepted an invitation from Mr. Jacob Mountain to become curate-in-charge of Blunham, Bedfordshire, where
he lived in the vicarage and worked harder than ever.

December 13. Commenced a cottage lecture at Charlton. Well
attended, but I fear they did not derive much good from coming
for I was cold and uninteresting, tho' God knows I endeavoured
to be otherwise.

His main activities consisted of two long Sunday sermons, a cottage lecture, a service in the poor house, teaching in the school
and instructing confirmation candidates. These efforts appear
to have been appreciated by his parishioners, for when in May
1833 he was appointed curate of All Souls, Langham Place, he
noted in his diary:

May. 11. Regret expressed by many of my poor brethren that I am
going to leave them. Much praise too of my sermons. They little
know what I am within and how much I have to humble me.

He commenced his London duties in September, lodging at 35 Castle Street on a stipend of £75 per annum; but at first experienced great difficulty in settling down in this large important parish, felt lonely, unhappy, and very much of a duck out of water. So much so that he contemplated accepting the offer of the two small Suffolk livings of Friston and Snape, which were offered him by a friend of the family, Colonel Vyse. However, he discovered in time that he would be expected to resign as soon as the colonel's younger son was ready for ordination. 'I am,' remarked the diarist, 'to hold for Eddy. Wrote to thank him and decline his offer.' Moreover he had now discovered an attractive reason for remaining in London.

February 1. 1834. Dined with Mrs. Smith. Began to feel an interest in that family beyond what is usual. May God guide me aright.

The Smiths, who were a wealthy and well-connected family, lived at 6 Portland Place, where the diarist became a frequent visitor. He began to communicate his hopes and fears to his journal:

I have been sometimes haunted by a dream of happiness, which is I fear entwining itself about my heart. May God enable me to keep it in proper subjection, and direct me aright in it, and save me from discontent and dissatisfaction with my lot.

On 27 April he preached a favourite sermon: 'There is a Friend that sticketh closer than a brother', and later commented: 'I have much felt of late the want of some earthly friend, some dear companion with whom I might enjoy the delights of mutual confidence. May God guide me aright in this and keep me contented though my lot remain unchanged.'

The pretty cause of all this emotional disturbance was Fanny Smith, one of several daughters, who was only too ready to respond to the attentions of so eligible a young suitor. Richard, nonetheless, was too shy either to approach her or her mother directly; and it was brother John who eventually went into action.

Something [wrote the diarist] should I believe be done. Oh! that nothing may be done by me that is not for her happiness as well as my own . . . May 6. An eventful day! my dearest brother John this morning made known to Mrs. S. my affection for Miss S., and stated my prospects. The day one of awful suspense, but my dear brother has just been here to shew me Mrs. S's reply after speaking to Miss S., and I think it more favourable than I had dared to anticipate. . . . May 7. Interview with Mrs. S. and afterwards alone with Miss S., when I had the happiness of hearing from herself that my affection is entirely returned.

He was now in the seventh heaven of delight; and a few days later had a further cause for rejoicing: 'May 13. Letter from the Bishop of Worcester offering me the living of Kinwarton. Could anything be more opportune?'

Seymour was collated to the Warwickshire rectory of Kinwarton on 29 May; and was married to Fanny at Mapledurham on 30 October, spending their honeymoon at 'The Vyne', the home of Mrs. Chute, which was kindly loaned them for the occasion. In November they settled into Kinwarton rectory and resolutely set about their life's work.

Robert Hart, who also kept a diary, became curate of Furneaux and Brent Pelham, Essex, in 1860; and subsequently served curacies at Gustingthorpe, Essex, Gillingham, Kent, and Great Maplestead, Essex, where he met and married Miss Katherine Sperling, the daughter of a deceased country solicitor, whose widow allowed the young married couple to have a set of rooms in her own spacious house, 'Monks'. At Great Maplestead Hart served under a vicar who was also a friend, Henry Corrie, and the diary gives full details of his manifold parish activities. He took regular services, classes for 'penitents', and gave communion at a House of Mercy for fallen women in the village, taught in the day-school, conducted confirmation classes, visited assiduously, studied voraciously and ran a night-school, where he found it difficult to enforce discipline: 'To night school in the evening, but the boys were so riotous that I could not keep it, so sent them home and broke up the school for a fortnight.' Here is a typical day's work:

January 11, 1868. To the House of Mercy at 9. Visited Argent, very ill, on my way back. Writing all a.m. After dinner I went out, visited Mrs. Butcher, B. Hart, Mrs. Curtis; called at several cottages: Mrs. Shearman, Mrs. Head, Mrs. Gray and Mrs. Cracknell. To the Church, the stove moved. Called at Argent's.

When not otherwise engaged he usually studied of an evening: 'read all the evening . . . in the evening sat reading with Kate'. Like Seymour he was most conscientious in sermon preparation:

January 8. Saturday. At my sermon all the morning . . . at my sermon all the evening. . . . March 7 . . . At my sermon all the evening till 11 p.m. . . . . March 11 . . . Finished my sermon in bedroom by 12.30 p.m.

Kate was a very active helpmate. She was musical and ran the choir: 'March 30. Dear Kate took choir girls to practice for Sunday morning at 6.30 p.m. She gets on so well.'

So hard indeed did they work that an all too frequent entry in the diary is 'very weary all day' or just 'very weary'.

His principal recreations were riding, fishing and croquet, of which last he was extremely fond and usually managed a game on most days during the spring and summer. On 15 April 1868 for instance, despite the fact that he had services at the House of Mercy at 9 a.m. and 6 p.m., taught in the school, took a confirmation class for an hour, and 'visited all p.m. with Kate', yet found 'time for croquet and to view a horse at Borley'. He fished with his brother-in-law, Arthur Spurgin, rector of Gresham in Norfolk. However, despite his apparently busy, happy life and the birth of a daughter, he was not satisfied with his position of subordination. After more than eight years in orders and at the age of thirty-five he was anxious for a living of his own, and sought an interview with his bishop, T. L. Claughton of St. Albans, at Chelmsford on 14 September 1868: 'Walked to the Deanery.

Lunched with the Bishop . . . he was so kind. I told him of my discomfort here. He walked me round the park and sent me to the train.' Claughton was a good friend and benefactor to Robert Hart throughout his life, and the first fruits of this affection was seen in the offer of a benefice :

November 3. House of Mercy at 9 a.m. A letter from the Bishop offering me the Vicarage of Takeley, Essex. I am overwhelmed thereby . . . November 4. To London with Kate by the early train . . . to Bishop-Stortford by 11 a.m. train, then by fly to Takeley Vicarage. Saw over house, church, and school with Mr. Tufnell the present Vicar, who is a very ill man. Slept at the George at Bishop-Stortford and wrote all evening.

The following day he wrote to the bishop to accept the living; and in the Spring of 1869 he, Kate, and their baby daughter, Lilla, moved to Takeley. But before they went they wound up their work at Great Maplestead with a splendid school treat, for which Arthur Spurgin provided them with a magic lantern, the newest toy :

January 13, 1869. To the Vicarage to see and arrange with Mrs. Corrie and Miss Wren about the School Treat. B. Hawkins came to help with lantern sheet etc. . . . to School at 5 p.m. 64 children. Exhibited magic lantern and had two dishes of snapdragons which gave immense pleasure. Kate gave little presents to her children. After 3 cheers, broke up at 9 p.m. Parents came to see lantern.

But probably the best known diarist of them all is Francis Kilvert, who was curate of Clyro in Radnorshire and under his father at Langley Burrell, Wiltshire; although his diary, so unexpectedly stumbled upon by William Plomer and published in the late 1930s, is too well known to need summarising in any detail. This diary, originally compiled in twenty-two note-books, covers the period from 1870 to 1879 and is written in a simple, vivid, beautiful prose that at times verges upon poetry. 'Why,' he asked himself, 'do I keep this voluminous journal?' And replied : 'because life appears to me such a curious and wonderful thing.' Out of it there emerges the portrait of a curate of good family, who happily devoted his short life—he died of peritonitis at the early age of thirty-eight—and remarkable natural gifts to an obscure country ministry, where he was greatly beloved by all his parishioners, especially the very old and the very young. He was at his best in a sick-room or a class-room. He possessed a deep personal religious faith that was completely divorced from party allegiances, and was highly successful in every form of pastoral work. He was a great walker and in his walks drank in the beauties of the countryside that he later confided to his journal in unforgettable prose. He had the mind of a poet, although the actual poetry he wrote was conventional and not very effective. On the other hand he was a man of no great intellectual attainments and suffered from some very ordinary human failings, notably a weakness for feminine charms and society. He has recorded for us the following amusing tale of a fellow-curate:

Thursday, April Eve, 1870. . . . In Hadley's shop I met Dewing who told me of a most extraordinary misfortune that befell Pope the curate of Cusop yesterday at the Whitney Confirmation. He had one candidate Miss Stokes a farmer's daughter and they went together by train. Pope went in a cutaway coat very short, with his dog, and took no gown. The train was very late. He came very late into church and sat on a bench with the girl cheek by jowl. When it came to his turn to present his candidate he was told by the Rector (Henry Dew) or someone in authority to explain why he came so late. The Bishop of Hereford (Atlay) has a new fashion of confirming only two persons at a time, kneeling at the rails. The Bishop had marked two young people come in very late and when they came up to the rails he thought from Pope's youthful appearance and from his having no gown that he was a young farmer candidate and brother of the girl. He spoke to them very severely and told them to come on and kneel down for they were extremely late. Pope tried to explain that he was a clergyman and that the girl was his candidate, but the Bishop was overbearing and imperious and either did not hear or did not attend, seeming to think he was dealing with a refractory ill-conditioned youth. 'I know, I know', he said. 'Come at once and kneel down, kneel down.' Poor Pope resisted a long time and had a long battle with the Bishop, but at last unhappily he was overborne in the struggle, lost his head, gave way, knelt down and was *confirmed* there and then, and no-one seems to have interfered to save him, though Mr. Palmer of Eardisley and others were sitting close by and the whole Church was in a titter. It is a most unfortunate thing and will never be forgotten and it will be unhappily a joke against Pope all his life. The Bishop was told of his mistake afterwards and apologised to Pope, though rather shortly and cavalierly. He said what was quite true that Pope ought to have come in his gown. But there was a little fault on all sides for if the Bishop had been a little less hasty, rough and overbearing in his manner things might have been explained, and the bystanding clergy were certainly very much to blame for not stepping forward and preventing such a farce. I fear poor Pope will be very much vexed, hurt and dispirited about it.

Another outstanding curate was the Reverend Samuel Earnshaw, who served as assistant minister at Sheffield parish church from 1847 until his death in 1888. Earnshaw was a fine scientist and mathematician as well as a distinguished theologian of broad views; but he is particularly remembered as the champion of the working classes. In a famous sermon on the Church and the Artisan he condemned the oppression of the poor by the rich and the use of religion to keep them in their place : 'an invention of the higher classes to keep the lower classes quiet and submissive'. Furthermore he derided the new and fashionable attempts to evangelise the urban masses by means of wholesale conversions at monster meetings : 'Working men will not go to these monster meetings, and people cannot be converted on a monster scale. . . . As long as we have only monster parishes there will be apathy and standing aloof of the people.' Instead he advocated small town benefices of not more than 400 houses, with small churches, where the parson could get to know his flock intimately, as happened in the country village. In his championship of the working man Earnshaw was not the only curate; the most noteworthy being the Reverend G. S. Bull, curate of Byerley near Bradford, who campaigned vigorously for many causes on their behalf : temperance reform, children's education, the Ten Hours Bill, and against the Poor Law Amendment Act of 1834. His short, thick-set figure was seen on a great number of platforms during the 'thirties and 'forties, where his sonorous voice, hard-headed common sense and boisterous humour commanded attention. Another was the Reverend C. B. Dunn, curate of Cumberworth in Yorkshire, who took a prominent part in the Co-operative Movement, for which he composed doggerel verses like the following.

> Let none who Christ's example court,
> Contend for sect or station,
> But all who human weal support,
> Support Co-Operation.

Finally, in concluding this section, one must not omit Nathaniel Woodard, the creator of the Woodard Schools, who was curate-in-charge of New Shoreham in Sussex for many years from 1848 onwards, where he began his great work of founding an organisation for providing a Church education for the middle classes on a large scale and in widely separated parts of the country.

By an Act of 1804, 44. George III. c. 43, the canonical ages of twenty-three for a deacon and twenty-four for a priest were to be strictly enforced. Previously it had not been unknown for men to be ordained into the diaconate at a very much earlier age. The examination of candidates for holy orders and their training for the ministry also gradually improved. Theological colleges came into existence. In 1800 there were none, but by 1874 ten or more were flourishing; although even then they only catered for a minority of ordinands, who attended for a few terms. Others might go and live with an incumbent for some months before ordination in order to have their reading supervised for the coming diocesan examination and also to gain a little experience of parochial work. Others again might remain longer at the university to attend divinity lectures. But the vast majority simply went home after taking their degree and whiled away the time as best they could until they reached the canonical age. Residence at a university and the gaining of a degree were regarded as a perfectly adequate preparation for the ministry. Practical parochial experience would be gained in their first curacy at the expense

of the unfortunate parishioners. Examinations were often super-
ficial. The chaplain and son-in-law of Bishop North (1771–1820)
once examined two candidates for orders at a cricket match while
waiting to go in to bat; and the chaplain of Bishop Douglas
(1787–1807) did so as he was shaving. When Charles Perry,
Fellow of Trinity College, Cambridge, was ordained deacon in
1833, the bishop of Gloucester, J. H. Monk, received him 'with a
courteous bow' and the remark : 'It would be superfluous, Mr.
Perry, to examine a gentleman of your well-known acquirements'.
Archbishop Harcourt of York was particularly notorious in this
respect. In his one interview with a candidate in 1833 he said :
'Well, Mr. Sharp, so you are going to be curate to your father,
Mr. Sharp of Wakefield. Make my compliments to him when you
go home. My secretary has your testimonials; he will give you
full instructions. Be sure to be at the Minster in good time. Good
morning.' He is also reported to have said to his nephew, who
was being ordained to a family living, 'I think it will save both
you and me some trouble if I shoot through both barrels; so I
will ordain you both deacon and priest this afternoon'. When
E. B. Ellman was to be ordained deacon in 1838 by the bishop
of Lincoln in Buckden Parish Church on letters dimissory from
the bishop of Chester, he had first to travel into South Wales in
order to persuade a reluctant chaplain on holiday there, to set
him an examination paper before the ordination. At his interview with Bishop Bathurst of Norwich, William Andrew was
grilled about the life of his prospective rector, and when he
refused to answer the bishop rose in anger and said : 'You don't
know what you come for, sir !' and dismissed him. This looked
ill for his hopes of ordination; but he was fortunate in that a
friend of his, Mr. Newton, knew the bishop's chaplain and introduced them. So 'the questions of that day passed off agree-
ably'. However, the bishop objected to his latin theme, although
there was nothing grammatically wrong with it, and it was only
with great difficulty that he persuaded the chaplain, Mr. Drake,
to allow him to write another. This passed muster and he was told,

'That will do very well, sir. You will present yourself for ordination tomorrow.' But the service itself was far from satisfactory: during which some of his fellow-candidates tittered and behaved irreverently. Afterwards many of them repaired to the Maid's Head for an unseemly celebration.

Another curate whose vicar was *persona non grata* with the bishop, and who suffered accordingly, was Peter Young of Hursley in Hampshire, where John Keble the notorious Tractarian was incumbent. The Bishop of Winchester, who disapproved strongly of Keble's theological opinions, vented his wrath on the curate when he presented himself for priest's orders in 1841. Keble ruefully admitted that he had undergone no examination whatever at his ordination to the priesthood, but Young was subjected to a very stringent one and finally rejected for his so-called unsound views on the question of the Real Presence of Christ in the Blessed Sacrament.

Such proceedings generally speaking became a thing of the past as the century wore on, although they lingered on in certain areas. E. W. Benson, who came for his examination into the diaconate at Manchester in 1853 was handed a document 'which had been lying sealed and directed upon a side table to the effect that he had passed a most creditable examination'; and when four years later he was to be priested at Ely he was informed that his examination was 'purely formal'. At Salisbury in 1845 under Bishop Thomas Burgess conditions were very different. 'He instituted a preliminary examination for candidates for deacon's orders to take place at Salisbury about three months previously to the ordination week. At this they were to appear personally and to bring with them a written syllabus or abridgement of certain prescribed books, such as Pearson 'On the Creed', Butler's 'Anthology', Burnet's 'History of the Reformation' and 'Pastoral Care'; and they were required to give proof of their qualifications for the performance of the public offices of the Church by reading aloud the Morning Service in the chapel before the bishop and his chaplain . . . his examination subsequently embraced a thorough acquaintance with the Bible, Ecclesiastical History, Evidences of Christianity, and the 39 Articles with their Scripture proofs.' He also demanded a knowledge of Hebrew; and saw to it that the candidate's sense of vocation and personal piety were thoroughly tested. Other bishops who led the way in enforcing a more careful preparation and searching examination were Henry Phillpotts of Exeter and Samuel Wilberforce of Oxford.

Most clergymen were still graduates of Oxford or Cambridge. Between 1834 and 1843 Oxford produced 2,076 deacons, Cambridge 2,307, while Dublin and Durham had only 302 between them, and some 565 came from other establishments. In the 1850s the average yearly Oxford contingent was about 200, with Cambridge slightly more, Dublin forty and other sources 110. Oxbridge, Dublin and Durham together provided 461 ordinands in 1874, against 194 others.

Various societies and organisations had come into being in order to help finance poor but suitable candidates. As early as 1773 the Evangelicals had started the Elland Clerical Education Society for this purpose; and later in 1795 the Bristol Clerical Education Society. The Creaton Clerical Education Society founded by Thomas Jones in 1812 enabled some fifty men from the Midlands to enter the ministry. Four years later these truly remarkable Evangelical ventures were capped by the formation of The London Clerical Education Society. But as the century went on many other similar organisations were established, notably the Clerical Education Aid Fund in 1845, by different sections of the Church.

However, it was not simply a question of encouraging men to take orders, but also of paying for their keep in the parishes to which they went. The large industrial towns in particular were crying out for curates, yet unable of themselves to find the money to support them. The Evangelicals again led the way by setting up the Church Pastoral Aid Society in 1836 for this purpose; but owing to its narrowly partisan approach to the problem it aroused much criticism. 'It was asked why an unofficial society should

test the opinion of a curate whom a bishop had agreed to licence.'
None the less it met a real need and by 1858 was spending nearly
£46,000 a year on maintaining curates and lay agents up and
down the country. In 1837 a High Church Group consisting of
Joshua Watson, Sir R. Inglis, M.P., and Benjamin Harrison
founded an opposition organisation under the name of the
Additional Curates' Society, which pledged itself to work only
through the bishops. Watson, who himself gave £500 and a
further £100 a year for the rest of his life, acted as honorary
treasurer and drew up the society's constitution. This stated
explicitly that 'no application for aid can be received by the
Committee, but through the Bishop of the diocese; or taken into
consideration without his previous sanction'; and he firmly laid
it down that no grants could be made to small country parishes,
or 'to entertain any cases in which the grant seemed likely to be
applied to the personal relief of the incumbent'. Grants, in fact,
were only given where it was reasonably certain that the addition
of another curate would mean more services, lectures and cate-
chetical instructions, or lead to a more systematical visitation of
the parishioners. Furthermore he insisted that any curate helped
by the society must be paid a reasonable salary, i.e. from £80 to
£100. By 1851 the Additional Curates' Society was assisting some
323 curates, and possessed an annual income of £19,000. The
Curates' Augmentation Fund was founded in 1866; but waited
two years in order to build up its capital before making any
grants. Then it began to augment the stipends of curates who
had served for fifteen years and were over forty years of age.
In 1876 the Secretary wrote : 'The object of the Fund is to provide increased stipends for curates who have served without
reproach for not less than fifteen years, and thus make it possible
for them to calculate on obtaining in middle life a professional
income sufficient to enable them to exercise their ministry without being harassed by pecuniary anxiety, or driven to seek the
aid of charitable institutions to obtain the necessaries of life. It
should, perhaps, be added that the number of curacies is so much

in excess of the benefices to which they can be promoted that a constantly increasing number have to wait twenty or thirty years before they obtain preferment, whilst many must remain curates all their lives. There are at present in active work as curates 1,060 men whose length of service exceeds fifteen years.' By 1900 this number had risen to 1,300. The grant in each case amounted to £50 per annum.

CHAPTER VII

The Twentieth-Century Curate

By the beginning of the present century it had become a very expensive matter to be ordained. Candidates were still expected to have taken a university degree; although this was a rule to which there were an increasing number of exceptions. But they were also strongly advised by the bishops to attend a post-graduate theological college for a year or more, whose charges varied from £70 to £170 per annum. Little help was available from central church funds; and despite the fact that both Mirfield and Kelham were now active in this field, it meant that most parents had to finance their own children through university and theological college to the tune of about £1,000 per head. In order to ease this situation the bishops agreed at the Lambeth Conference of 1908 to postpone compulsory residence at a theological college until 1917; but on the other hand they declared that after 1914 they would not accept any more candidates who did not have a university degree. Pressure was brought to bear upon Kelham to conform to this ruling, which however had to be abandoned after the First World War.

Yet even after such an expensive training the average assistant curate was fortunate if within a reasonable number of years he could obtain a living of his own, since there were still far more curates than benefices available to them. In 1900, for example, 1,300 applications were made to the Curates' Augmentation Fund; and by 1907 this figure had risen to 1,400. All too many curates in fact never became incumbents at all, but spent all their working lives as assistants. 'Nothing,' wrote an anonymous pamphleteer in the early 1900s, 'could be more discreditable to the

174

Church of England than the way she treats her unbeneficed clergy. At present the almost universal qualification for a benefice is the possession of private means. Hundreds of appointments are made on this sole recommendation. The unfortunate curate who does not possess any private means cannot accept a benefice. His lot in any Church but ours would still be a happy and honourable one. But it is notorious that with us his career is practically at an end at forty years of age; the Church which has impressed on him her indelible orders has no further need for his services.' None the less, although there were always something like 200 curates waiting for benefices, the country as a whole began to require many more clergy. In 1884, 814 new deacons were ordained, but by 1907 the number had dropped to 587 and continued to decline, which meant that the 7,000 curates then at work were not nearly enough to fill the gaps in view of the rapidly increasing population of England and Wales, especially in the industrial areas. More than 400 parishes were looking for one in vain. The Additional Curates' Society, which then supported some 1,400 parishes, found that between 1903 and 1907 from ten per cent to nineteen per cent of them were unable to take up their grants; while during the same period the Church Pastoral Aid Society had a very similar experience. Benefices with large staffs like Yarmouth, Portsea, Leeds, and Stepney, began to decrease in number, although the need for them was more apparent than ever. 'We sorely want,' wrote a St. Pancras pamphleteer, 'a few large Basilicas with a strong staff of five or six clergy, each carefully selected, not to be a sort of Jack of all trades, but for his particular vocation and ministry.' That was a dream which has not yet been realised; and in the meantime the 'Jack of all trades' continued to function, usually as a lonely assistant to his vicar.

The Evangelical and Oxford Movements had, however, by now so thoroughly permeated the Church that a new conception of service had been generally accepted by the clergy, who no longer regarded their profession as the means to a genteel way of life and a comfortable security, but rather as a vocation dedicated to the service of God and the extension of His Kingdom in whatever sphere of work was allotted to them. This was particularly true in Anglo-Catholic circles, where it became the fashion for newly-ordained curates to go into the slums, especially the East End of London and Dockland, rather than to accept a title in the better-class suburbs or the countryside. Here they might cheerfully and uncomplainingly remain all their working lives; some indeed in the very self-same parish to which they had originally been licensed; but always holding passionately to the splendid code of their kind: 'you asked for nothing—nothing whatever—you did what you were told, you went where you were sent, and you worked until you dropped'.

A headmaster at the Church Congress of 1908, talking about 'cruelty towards curates', exclaimed indignantly: 'The curate's position is hardly worth calling a position at all. It begins fairly well, it often ends in bitterness, disappointment and despair. He has no security of tenure. In theory he is the bishop's curate; but when friction arises, it is the exception for the curate to be supported.' Much depended, of course, on the kind of vicar one was working under. When Peter Green went to his first curacy at Lady Margaret Church, Walworth, he found the incumbent to be a most unpleasant eccentric, who took a violent dislike to him from the start and made his four years there a misery. He addressed Peter always as 'Green m'man', treated him as little better than a servant, and gave him all the hardest and nastiest jobs in the parish to perform, while making no attempt to train or help him in any way. Apparently he envied Peter his many gifts, and his jealousy rendered him tyrannical. During the diaconate it was then the custom to submit all written sermons to one's incumbent for criticism and advice. One Sunday morning the vicar actually preached the sermon that Peter Green had prepared for delivery that evening, and handed back the manuscript after the service with the words: 'Green m'man, you will have to get busy.' In the end there was a flare up; the bishop,

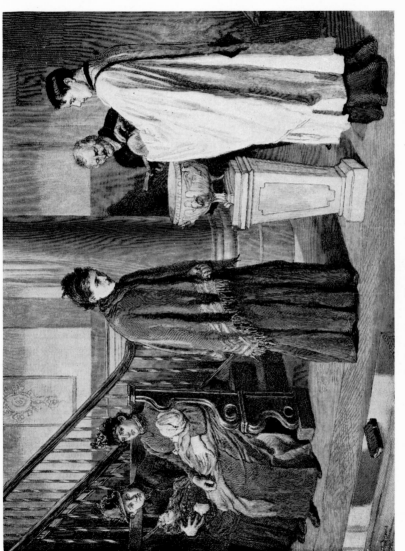

26.   A christening in the chapel of the Foundling Hospital.

27. The Rake's Progress : at the university 1806.

28. Rev. Robert Hart.

29. TRUE HUMILITY

Right Reverend Host. 'I'm afraid you've got a bad egg, Mr. Jones!'
The Curate. 'Oh no, my Lord, I assure you! Parts of it are excellent!'
From PUNCH 9 November 1895.

30. A PAN-ANGLICAN OVERSIGHT:
LAMBETH CONFERENCE 1867.
Anxious wife. 'Any help for our difficulties dear?'
Resigned husband. 'O no, love. We poor curates are not even mentioned!'
From PUNCH 19 October 1867.

Dr. E. S. Talbot, was called in and Peter left under a cloud. He went to Leeds parish church, where he was supremely happy. The vicar, Dr. E. S. C. Gibson, later bishop of Gloucester, gave him a splendid training as a curate and much help and direction in the matter of his theological reading. Dr. Gibson indeed thought so highly of him that he not only procured Peter Green his first living as rector of Sacred Trinity, Salford, but later recommended him for the bishopric of New Guinea. In the few 'large Basilicas' like Leeds and Portsea the work might be hard and the discipline tough, but you were sure of a first-class grounding in the priesthood and of good future prospects in the Church. Such parishes were in fact stepping-stones to high promotion. Curates like Lang, Garbett, and J. G. Simpson were certainly 'going places'.

But it was often far otherwise for the single curate in the ordinary industrial, surburban or country parish. For most town parsons were busy men who tended to think of their new assistant simply in terms of the amount of work that could be unloaded onto him, rather than to regard him as a friend and a colleague and try to prepare the young man for his future ministry. As likely as not he would pour cold water on his curate's naïve enthusiasms, of which he was half-afraid, and clamp down upon him a rigid discipline in accordance with his own conceptions of right and wrong. The result too often was an unhappy relationship, with the incumbent eyeing his colleague to see that he did not overstep the mark, and his young curate hotly resenting what he regarded as an intolerable discipline and subjection. One such assistant used regularly to sigh with relief when he heard his vicar taking his boots off in the bedroom of the clergyhouse immediately above him. There was peace at last! In the country there were still incumbents who employed curates to do all the work while they sat back and took life easily. The Reverend H. Fiennes-Clinton, a relative of the duke of Newcastle, who was rector of Cromwell in Nottinghamshire, a village of not more than 150 souls, was such a man. His curate, C. W. Knox, was kept with his nose to the grindstone, while the rector lived the life of the country gentleman proper to his station. But not all incumbents were like that. One of the fruits of the nineteenth-century spiritual revival was to give to the clergy a greater sense of partnership in their task of extending Christ's kingdom, and in a growing number of parishes before the First World War incumbent and curate worked happily together in an atmosphere of brotherly co-operation rather than on the basis of employer and employed. Livings, however, were hard to come by. Anxious to retain their curates at a time when the supply of ordinands was running short, vicars were often unsympathetic or urgent in their appeals that men should stay where they were. Diocesan authorities and private patrons were equally hard to convince that merit and length of service entitled one to an independency. 'It is quite a mistake,' A. F. Webling, curate of a Portsmouth parish, was told by a friend, 'to suppose that in the Church of England as by law established, merit automatically meets its reward. It is necessary for merit to get on a tub and draw attention to itself with piercing cries. The Crown is patron of a large number of livings. Place your name on the waiting-list for anything suitable that may become vacant.' To which his archdeacon added the advice : 'you must watch the weekly clerical obituary, and as each suitable Crown living falls vacant, you must apply for it and bring to bear all the influence you can command to support your endeavour.' By the beginning of the twentieth century a curate would be earning between £120 and £150 per annum; and on an average an 'independency' might come his way, if ever, after a dozen years. But the older he got the less hope he had of obtaining a benefice, or even of securing any new employment, if for one reason or another he should lose his present post. For despite a growing shortage of ordinands the elderly curate was not a welcome substitute. He was either too independent-minded or else too set in his ways; his seniority demanded a higher scale of remuneration, but his physique prevented him from undertaking successfully the hard unpleasant tasks which could be safely allocated to a younger man; and above all his experience and age might constitute him a formidable rival to the incumbent in the respect or affections of the parishioners.

Moreover, quite apart from the possibility of instant dismissal at the whim of a sitting incumbent, against which there was little hope of a successful appeal to the bishop who had licensed him, an assistant was sure to have to go when the benefice changed hands, after performing the arduous task of running the parish on his own during the sequestration. An incoming incumbent almost invariably made a clean sweep of his predecessor's curates, casting them out into the world to sink or swim. There was no pension; a curate did not qualify for help from the Victoria Clergy Fund; and he had no vote or place in convocation where he might plead his cause. No wonder a curate at the Church Congress of 1908 roundly condemned a system 'which allowed it to be possible for a man in holy orders some twenty-seven years to be ousted from his sphere of work by incoming incumbents no less than five times during such a period; accompanied indeed with expressions of goodwill and best wishes; yet the act is done'. After the age of fifty he became practically unemployable. What happened to him then? In his short story *The Dream*, H. G Wells paints a picture of such a man and his wife, the Reverend Mr. and Mrs. Moggeridge. They had retired to the second floor of a seedy lodging-house in Pimlico, where they eked out a miserable existence. Their landlady described them to her friend as follows:

A very poor clergyman, but a clergyman. So much to our credit, Martha. Oh! but they're poor old things! Poor old things! Been curate or something all his life in some out-of-the-world place. And lost his job. Somebody had the heart to turn 'em out. Or something happened. I wonder. 'E's a funny old man. . . . He dodders off nearly every Saturday on supply, they call it, to take service somewhere over Sunday and like as not he comes back with his cold worse than ever, sniffing. It's cruel how they treat these poor old parsons on supply, fetch 'em from the station in open traps they do, in the worst of weather, and often the rectory teetotal without a drop of anything for a cold. Christianity! I suppose it's got to be. . . . The two of them just potter about upstairs and make shift to get their meals, such as they are, over the bedroom fire. She even does a bit of her own washing. Dragging about. Poor old things! Old and forgotten and left about. But they're very little trouble and there it is. And as I say—anyhow—he's a clergyman.

Gradually the position improved. At last by the Patronage Measure of 1930 curates secured representation in convocation provided they totalled one-third of all the clergy in one diocese; and as their numbers declined their bargaining power increased.

During the First World War the supply of men to be ordained dried up completely; and although a tremendous effort was made immediately afterwards to train ex-army personel at Knutsford, the numbers remained small for many years to come. At least 550 deacons were needed per annum to make up the deficiency; yet between 1920 and 1930 those entering the ministry rarely rose above 400 a year, and it was not until 1932 that the annual wastage figure of 550 was passed, after which the numbers rose steadily and in 1939, immediately before the Second World War, 590 men were ordained. The shortage of these years is reflected in the pages of Crockford, where, in volume after volume, the anonymous author bewails the scarcity of curates. In 1924 he wrote : 'In most parishes the Assistant curate is already one of the rarer migrants, and he promises to become before long as scarce as the bittern or the bustard'; and added seven years later : 'The situation is still going from bad to worse.' Furthermore the type of man now entering the ministry was very different from the pre-war ordinand. He came from a lower social class with a less sheltered economic background, but with a greater experience of life and a tougher personality. The growing social problems of the inter-war years, culminating in mass unemployment, fired the imagination of a robust type of young man, including ex-service men, who, at a time when the Welfare State was still very much in its infancy, felt that they had a vocation for social service, for which the Church offered a field of opportunity. Fewer and fewer were from good public schools or from Oxford and Cambridge; and intellectual and educational standards were often low, since a number of bishops who, with the aid of their examining chaplains, were still solely responsible for the selection of candidates, were notoriously lax in this respect, notably William Temple and Winnington Ingram.

With this new type of man entering the ministry great efforts were made by the Church as a whole to give him financial assistance in his training. Many individual dioceses established funds for this purpose; while C. A. C. T. M. (The Central Advisory Council on the Training for the Ministry) had been set up as early as 1913 to make grants to carefully selected candidates, although it did not at this stage act as a vetting instrument for ordinands as a whole.

The laws of demand and supply operating in a field of shortage ensured that from the newly fledged deacon to the senior curate the unbeneficed had a better deal than ever before. Their stipends ranged on the average from £200 to £250 per annum, together with the free use of rooms in a clergyhouse or a free house for a married man; they were less subservient to their employers, since once they were licensed they could only be dismissed after six months notice with the approval of the bishop, which was not always easy to obtain. In any case incumbents were loath to part with a curate, unless for exceptional reasons, since it became ever harder to replace him. The curate on the other hand could now move about much more freely and easily. Parishes were crying out for assistant priests of any kind and incumbents were not above poaching their neighbours' preserves, luring young men away with the bait of higher incomes and better conditions. However, in the 1930s there was a set back, at least in the Midlands and north of England, owing to the economic blizzard. Parishes that in the 'twenties had employed several curates with relatively high incomes, now found it harder and harder to support one; while many gave up the struggle altogether and left the vicar to carry on single-handed. Northern bishops had to become very cautious of accepting for ordination even the most suitable of men, since so few parishes were now available to employ them. In 1933, for instance, the three Lancashire dioceses of Manchester, Liverpool and Blackburn ordained only sixty-seven men between them. Consequently many candidates, who had exhausted their resources in obtaining their training and were unable to wait any longer, were forced into taking teaching or other secular jobs wherever they could be found, or else accept a title from the 'wrong' type of incumbent, who alone could afford to employ them.

After the First World War the need to train ordained men began to be recognised by authority as a moral duty owed to them by the Church; and pressure was brought to bear upon incumbents, with varying success, to put it into practice on a much wider scale than ever before. Famous parishes like Portsea and Leeds had long adopted this policy; and the discipline and experience gained there by a succession of assistant priests had proved invaluable for their future careers, turning out large numbers of remarkable men. At St. Mary's, Portsea, indeed, under Cyril Garbett the discipline had been ferocious; obedience was the keynote and woe betide the idle or inefficient curate. Before the War there were some fifteen of them living together at the Vicarage. Their days were mapped out to the last minute : study in the mornings, four hours visiting in the afternoons and more visiting or club-work in the evenings. 'Compline was at 10.15 a.m. The rest of the day was our own.' These men all came to Portsea as deacons from Oxford and Cambridge and stayed there until they married or obtained a living. One of them, Oswald Hunt, was curate from 1904 to 1920. For their first two years at Portsea they had every Monday morning to submit to the vicar an account of how they had spent every hour of the preceding week, excluding their day off, and what books they had read. The pay was poor : £110 for a deacon, of which £80 was deducted for his keep, and £120 for a priest; the food was plain and inadequate; and the whole set-up was rigidly despotic. Garbett himself could be terrifying. He once said to Tubby Clayton, who had changed the time of his boys' club from 7 p.m. to 7.30 p.m. without asking permission, when the vicar was due to visit them, '*You* have altered the time! Are *you* correcting my whole time-table? I supposed it has not occurred to you that I have other things to do tonight?' When the Reverend A. Cory was discovered mending a colleague's motor cycle in the vicarage garden after 2.30 p.m., Garbett told him: 'You weren't ordained to do that sort of thing: get down to your district.' Mealtimes at Portsea could be most uncomfortable occasions. When Garbett came in there would be a sudden hush and afterwards the curates' chatter was subdued. C.F.G. was certainly not loved; but if he was feared he was also respected and admired by all his curates, even though they could never give him that personal devotion enjoyed by his predecessor, Bernard Wilson. None the less he inspired tremendous loyalty—woe betide the man who was not loyal!—for his own example was an inspiration in itself. Forty years later one of his old curates wrote: 'There was no reason why one should not say one's daily offices or one's simple prayers as regularly and as faithfully as he did; no reason why one should not visit as relentlessly as he did, nor prepare one's sermons as carefully as he did, nor answer one's letters as promptly. Such shortcomings were not due to one's lack of gifts, but to our failure to use the gifts we had, and C.F.G. was a perpetual challenge to us to do as he did and use our gifts more fully. . . . His greatness lay in his perpetual demonstration of the art of the spiritually simple.' Garbett was certainly not the ogre he is sometimes represented to be. No one could be more kind to his curates when they got themselves into serious trouble; he saw to it that they had their regular day off a week and good long summer holidays; and above all he gave them their heads and allowed them to develop their natural abilities to the full, whether as scholar, athlete, mystic or administrator. 'Although the set-up was rigid and the discipline fierce,' declared yet another of his curates, 'we were *told* very little . . . C.F.G. had no use for a man who faithfully did what he was told, but not much else.' Certainly he never had any difficulty in obtaining curates. The famous Portsea training appealed strongly to high-spirited young ordinands, many of of whom had already suffered an apprenticeship at their public schools in 'fagging' for despotic seniors. Furthermore it constituted a challenge to their manhood, an opportunity to serve Christ under the toughest conditions; and it bred some remarkable men.

Leeds parish church had a much longer tradition of this sort of thing, since whereas the Portsea experiment had only really begun with Edgar Jacob in 1878, that at Leeds dated back to 1837 and Dr. Hook's famous ministry. The training of the curates was much the same, there was the same comradeship, enthusiasm, hard and continuous work, and a sense of a privileged status that took the form of wearing top-hats and frock coats in order to distinguish them from the ordinary run-of-the-mill curate; but it was mellower and lacked the ferocious discipline and rigid obedience which Garbett imposed and expected. For one thing the vicar was a married man and lived in his vicarage, while his curates inhabited a clergyhouse down the road. They were continually in one another's company, but they never got quite so on top of one another as at Portsea. The relationship was more of a father to his children than a despot towards his slaves. Edward Stuart Talbot, who became vicar in 1888, used to invite two or three of his curates once a week to the vicarage at 7.30 a.m. to read with him for an hour from 'the Fathers' over a cup of coffee. One can hardly imagine Garbett doing anything of that kind! Cosmo Lang, who served his one and only curacy at Leeds in the early 1890s recalled a vivid example of the kind of zealous enthusiasm displayed by the Leeds' curates at that time, with the fatherly encouragement of their Vicar:

With the ardour of youth I had at once set my heart on living in the midst of the poor folk who surrounded the Parish Church. One who had as a layman enthused about University Settlements could scarcely as a parson be content to live elsewhere. Simpson (J. G. Simpson) and an elder curate known as Father Marks promised to join me. The other curates were very sniffy about our project, but the Vicar smiled upon our zeal. The difficulty was to get any sort of house in what was then a very derelict quarter of Leeds. At last an old public-house, which had been deprived of its licence, was secured. It was placed most conveniently, at the end of old Church Row. But other conveniences besides that of site there were none. The public bar-room (retaining the bar) became our refectory, the more private bar-parlour, with its stone floor became at first my study. My bedroom, which was never carpeted, was over one of the single rooms which abounded in that district, where tramp-folk lodged at sixpence a night. I used often to be disturbed by the oaths and screams of quarrelsome couples below. I once found in that room in utter squalor a man who had been a boy at Eton. 'I was then, I've been ever since a drifter', so he said, 'and I've drifted down to this'. After a year I migrated to another small house next door—so small that it had been condemned as a dwelling-house— a groundroom which could just hold a writing table, a small book-case and two chairs, which was my study, an upper room for a bedroom (uncarpeted), containing an iron bedstead (on which I slept even at Bishopthorpe!), a small wash-stand, a chair and a tin bath. There was no bathroom in either house. This bedroom was so low that I could just stand upright within it and no more. This was my home for nearly three years, and I found it quite sufficient.

Outside he visited in the slum districts of Kirkgate and Marsh Lane, an area of squalid hovels where most of the women were prostitutes, and where he often had to interfere with fierce fights. He started a home for the parentless boys who then abounded in the town, the sellers of matches and newspapers; and he visited regularly in the Leeds Infirmary.

Another centre for curate training was St. Helens, Lancashire, the largest town in the diocese of Liverpool, with four mission churches, five or six clergy, Church Army captains and lady workers. It made its name under three brilliant vicars: J. W. Willink, later Dean of Norwich, C. C. B. Bardsley, later Bishop of Peterborough and Leicester, and Albert Baines, later Arch-deacon of Wakefield; and became a recognised training ground for promising young men destined for preferment. The discipline was as strict as in the more famous establishments, the work as hard and continuous, and the same uniform was worn : frock coats and silk hats. When Gresford Jones, later Bishop of St. Albans, joined the parish as a curate, he was sent by the vicar to the York Street area, who told him 'that apart from the staff meetings and statutory services in the Parish Church he did not wish to see him again for three months. But then he would expect a case history of every family in that area.' One of the better-known curates was Christopher Chavasse, the son of the Bishop of Liverpool, who went there as a deacon in 1910. At first he was very much under his vicar's eye and had to submit all his sermons to him for approval. But when at length this rule was relaxed an amusing episode took place. Chavasse had had a busy week and was playing an away match for St. Helen's rugby team on the Saturday, so he was unable to prepare a sermon. But passing through Liverpool on his way home from the match he called at the palace and borrowed one of his father's. After he had delivered it the next day, Bardsley commented : 'I have heard you preach some bad sermons in the past year, Chavasse, but that was the worst.' After being priested he was put in charge of the York Street Mission, where drunkenness was the great social evil. So he started a Saturday morning concert followed by a hot meal and then persuaded as many as possible to come and see him play rugby—as a player he was almost up to international standard—thus delaying the drinking until late in the evening. This was the time for parish visits. Led by the vicar the clergy and lay-workers visited all the public houses at 11 p.m. and invited all the men and women, most of them very drunk, to the mission hall, where they were given hot food and drink and listened to a gospel message. Chavasse, it was said, always arrived with a drunk on either arm. Often it was only in the early hours that the clergy could escape to their own beds, with a busy Sunday looming ahead of them. Intensive visiting, the founding and running of clubs for all ages and both sexes, and the conducting of Sunday schools and Bible classes, were the curates' main activities, most of whom would stay in the parish for at least seven years.

Among the lesser publicised industrial parishes a splendid example of the right type of curate-training was to be found at St. Philip's, Salford, under Canon Peter Green. Green began by giving a curate his head. 'An assistant curate,' writes Edward Carpenter, 'ought to be left sufficiently free to develop along the lines of his God-given particularity; and a wise vicar will both recognise and foster this development.' Canon Green did just that. His new recruit was allocated a particular part of the work of the parish and allowed to get on with it without interference for several months. Then, as one of his curates later wrote : 'After three months there came a casual question whether one could spare time for a chat, and at the appointed time he politely tapped on one's door, and asked if he might come in and sit down. What I came to regard as the Quarterly Review then started. He began by saying how extraordinarily well you were doing, followed by the inevitable 'but'. The fact generally emerged that, far from being unnoticing, he had missed nothing. He proceeded to take you to pieces with the skill and gentleness of a loving anatomist. Perhaps it is truer to say that he led you to do it for yourself, for there was no suggestion of delivering a lecture. He got you going over the ground for yourself—the visiting of the people you had got to know; the workers in this or that organisation, your general ideas, intentions and hopes; the methods of preparation for sermons and addresses, and the difficulties and problems encountered, what you were reading and whether it was congenial, and so on . . . for the most part it was all pleasant and easy going, and it was not until he had gone off with some final words of appreciation and encouragement that you realised how completely he had emptied you and revealed you to yourself. He continued this method for about two years, after which he felt that a man was sufficiently fledged for it to be needed no longer.' He was especially careful to encourage his curates in their theological reading; and his rule was that at least four mornings a week should be spent in study; while at mealtimes in his clergyhouse he almost invariably talked books. 'He did most of the Manchester Guardian reviews,' declared another curate, 'and he would frequently push a book across at one at breakfast and ask one's opinion of it. . . . But the talk was not always theological. He had an amazingly wide knowledge of literature of every type . . . and if one attempted a quotation and got a word wrong it was corrected at once.' He always listened attentively to his curates' sermons, praising and criticising them in a friendly way, but demanding chapter and verse for any particularly outrageous or unusual statement of fact. He told the candidates at ordination retreats : 'Keep up your reading, and make a subject of your own and study it as if you were going to write a book on it. You may never write the book, but that will not matter.' Here indeed was curate-training at its best and without tears; and the men subjected to it became Canon Green's staunchest friends and most admiring disciples. When one day at tea a curate confessed apologetically that instead of going visiting he had slept all the afternoon, Peter Green smilingly replied : 'Well, I expect you needed it.' Garbett would have let fly!

In all too many parishes, however, particularly where the curate was a lone wolf, his training was often of the sketchiest, and sometimes still is! He was simply pitchforked into the parish and left to get on with it. A contributor to *The Church Times* as late as 11 October 1968 wrote: "I have many hair-raising stories of friends who, on arrival in their new parishes, have been expected to do all the visiting and all the youth work with no past records to go on, and to prepare a sermon each Sunday without any help from the incumbent. In one case the boss put his feet firmly on the mantelpiece and went to sleep for three months! Others have been no more than messenger boys to the incumbent.'

Fashions were changing in other ways. Not only were newly fledged ordinands now opting for the town parish and particularly the slum, rather than the country village as of yore; but began to parade a muscular christianity in place of the erstwhile image of the effeminate 'pale young curate' beloved by the Victorian maiden lady and run after by all her nieces. But curates were discouraged from marriage. Archbishop Lang used to advise them to wait for at least five years, thereby accumulating capital and experience and possibly a living of their own before plunging into matrimony. Consequently in most parishes there was still no house for the curate; he was expected either to live in the clergyhouse, lodge at the vicarage or find himself digs. A knowledge of boxing was considered valuable, especially in the slums. Peter Green boxed at Cambridge, and in his first curacy at Walworth stood up to the 'Fighting Tinman' in the parish boxing-booth for the regulation five minutes, survived and was awarded a prize. This training stood him in good stead when he came upon a man beating his wife in the street and ordered him to desist. 'Orl right, then,' replied the tough, 'I'll 'it the bloody parson.' But after a second look at this particular parson he wisely refrained from doing so. A Bradford curate visiting one of the less desirable homes in his parish suddenly found himself facing a shut door, an ox of a man and a demand to hand over his gold watch. As it happened this cleric had won his boxing blue at Cambridge, so he took his watch from his pocket, laid it on the table, and gave his host exactly a minute to move aside and let him pass. Later he had occasion to visit his would-be assailant in hospital. When Christopher Chavasse, later Bishop of Rochester, first started a Bible class at his York Street Mission in St. Helens parish, he found a group of young toughs outside, who had come to make trouble. He invited them in. 'No one will ever get me in,' declared one of them. 'If I do,' asked Chavasse, 'will you promise to attend regularly?' The youngster laughed and promised. Whereupon Christopher seized hold of him, flung him over his shoulder and carried him kicking and shouting into the hall. The treatment was effective for this particular boy became one of Christopher's best youth leaders.

Perhaps because of their own traditionally precarious position, low wages, long hours and sometimes tyrannical masters, together with that urge to revolt against the Establishment, which was beginning to bite the youth of the post-war years and has reached such tremendous proportions in our own day, many curates, especially in the industrial areas, were socialists; and their sympathy with the unemployed and strikers of the 'twenties and 'thirties was often expressed injudiciously, loudly and vociferously, thereby endangering their own security. An incumbent of a fashionable London suburb taking a well-earned sabbatical leave and putting his assistant in charge of the parish during his absence, returned to find the church emptied of its well-to-do pew-holders and filled instead by the riff-raff of the neighbourhood. So his first reaction was to sack the offending curate. Another clerical firebrand sent to preach in a conservative village, stared down from the pulpit at the squire peacefully slumbering below him and thundered forth : 'I believe in calling a spade a spade.' Whereupon the squire awoke with a start and replied equally emphatically, 'And I say One no Trumps.' The Anglo-Catholics in particular were the champions of the workers; and slum curates in the East End of London and elsewhere were conspicuous for getting the poor to attend their churches by the combination of a colourful ritualism with a fiery socialism. Yet even their success was only partial; for despite the great champions of christian socialism like Percy Dearmer, Stuart Headlam, Charles Marson, Canon Donaldson and Father Adderley, the mass of the workers were still alienated by clerical stress on the authority of the Church. For they wished to think for themselves, to assert their own independence, and were largely indifferent to the Church as an historical institution. Moreover most Englishmen were natural Protestants, and the evangelical clergy were more interested in the salvation of the soul than the nourishment of the body.

By and large, then, the assistant curate was finding his feet between the two World Wars. No longer was he a slave at his master's beck and call; no longer could he be humiliated with impunity; and no longer was he the unconsidered clerical drudge, who could be cast out at a moment's notice. His position was secure, his standard of living was rising rapidly, and he was not afraid to assert his independence, conscious of his bargaining power and probable episcopal support. The relationship between incumbent and assistant took on a new and different complexion. The vicar was now chary of ordering his colleague about without explanation as if he were a kind of superior servant, but began instead to consult him as an equal, to confide in him as a friend, and to take his advice and ideas seriously. They were sometimes on christian name terms and the older man would often take an active interest in his curate's future. Livings were far easier to come by; and instead of having to wait twelve or fifteen years for his first independency, most young priests could expect a benefice after about six years' service. The curate who desired but never acquired one at all, had practically disappeared. The stage was set for the next leap forward, or backward.

CHAPTER VIII

Conclusion (1945-69)

During and immediately after the Second World War there was again a great shortage of ordination candidates. Between 1938 and 1949 the number of curates in the Manchester diocese dropped from 141 to 54; those in Liverpool from 158 to 58; in Sheffield from 106 to 43; in York from 122 to 54; and in Birmingham from 178 to 38. Soon after the war the Bishop of London wrote: 'We have been ordaining two or three men, not many more, at our ordination services in the last few years . . . it will be a long time before we go back to the fifty or sixty at each ordination which used to be characteristic of this diocese.'

In 1945 only 159 deacons were ordained; but ten years later the figure had risen to 446, after which there was a steady increase until the peak year of 1963 when 636 men received deacon's orders. Since that date, however, there has been an equally steady decline. 1967 produced only 496 deacons; and there was a further drop of seventeen in 1968. The Annual Report of the Advisory Council for the Church's Ministry in this latter year makes it clear that whereas from 1950 to 1962 the number of new ordinands roughly kept pace with the increasing population,* since that time there were not nearly enough deacons forthcoming to fill the gaps caused by natural wastage, let alone increase the overall number of the parochial clergy; particularly in view of the population explosion which was then taking place. The population of England and Wales in 1962 was 46.7 million and continues to rise on an average of 870,000 births per annum. By the end of the century this birth rate may possibly have grown

---

* 'Although,' states the report, 'this could only be interpreted as a "catching-up" on the inevitable "war-time decrease".'

31. MISUNDERSTOOD

Mrs Van de Leur. 'By the way, Mr Fairfax, if any of my son's old boots would be of use to you . . .'

Mr Fairfax (interrupting). 'Really, Madam! The clergy *are* underpaid but we can . . .'

(Rises to take his leave. But Mrs Van de Leur was only thinking of the Ragged School.)

From PUNCH 30 April 1898.

32. *Curate* (who struggles to exist on £120 a year with wife and six children). 'We are giving up meat as a little experiment, Mrs Dasher.'

Wealthy Parishioner. 'Oh, yes! One can live *so well* on fish, poultry, game and plenty of nourishing wines, can't one?'

From PUNCH 3 March 1909.

33. Curate writing a sermon in his lodgings 1905.

34.   A country parson 1907.

35.   Curate officiating at Holy Communion in a private house.

36. An industrial chaplain.

into the region of two million. Furthermore it is most unevenly distributed. Some country districts are hardly increasing at all, whereas the Midlands, London and the South East are developing at an alarming rate. These latter areas are especially in need of curates, who remain in tragically short supply. The report of the Archbishop's Committee set up in 1957 to investigate the distribution of ordination candidates, which was later amended by the Bishop of Birmingham, estimated in June 1962 that some 4,921 curates were needed to meet this situation, but only 2,579 were then at work; and it was also established by this investigation 'that curates tend to flow into southern areas of relative success as against the conurbations and northern areas of greatest needs.' Heavily populated dioceses such as London, Manchester and Birmingham were and still are so short of curates that their bishops could have placed hundreds of assistants had they been available.

Other factors were likewise making their presence felt. Owing to a general shortage of clergy, curates no longer remained curates for any length of time. At the beginning of the century a man was lucky if he was promoted to a benefice of his own after a dozen years' service; by the 1920s and 1930s a minimum of six years was the average; but after the last war most priests could expect a living when they had been four or five years in orders, sometimes as little as three. Consequently the larger town parishes and the new group ministries, which were then just coming into existence, that depended upon a staff of curates for their efficient maintenance, found themselves continually having to replenish them in a highly competitive market. The Portsea or Leeds curate, who stayed ten years or more in his first job, was now an anachronism.

Another source of wastage were the specialised ministries which are attracting many curates into their ranks after a few years in parish work. For a general impression is now growing among the younger clergy in the Church of England that the long established parochial system with its independent single benefices

N

193

THE CURATE'S LOT

run by jacks-of-all-trades has had its day, and that the future
lies either with the new group ministeries or else in these specialised extra-parochial ministeries designed to meet particular needs,
which include the new mass media of radio, television and journ-
alism, great communal centres like factories, prisons, hospitals, the
fighting-services, schools and youth organisations, the various
boards and commissions set up by the Church Assembly, and the
Church's many societies at home and overseas. And of these two
it is the latter rather than the parochial ministry that seems to
offer them both better prospects of promotion and to show more
tangible results for their labours.

More and more clergy are coming to ordination in middle life—
the A.C.C.M. Report, quoted above, noted that between 1963
and 1966 'there was a sharp drop in all age groups except for men
over forty',* which meant of course that their term of service
was inevitably greatly curtailed. Since the last war parents are no
longer expected to foot the bill for a son who has been accepted
for ordination and sent to university and theological college. That
is now the combined responsibility of State and Church. All candidates are expected to attend a theological college, of which
there are twenty-seven situated up and down the country,† (a
college for older men at Worcester closed in July 1969) and a
training course established in the Southwark diocese to enable
working men to read for Holy Orders in their spare time. They
must first, however, be accepted for ordination, after stringent
testing, by C.A.C.T.M.—now A.C.C.M., i.e. The Advisory Council for the Church's Ministry—which since the 1940s has taken
over the task from the episcopate of vetting all candidates. Those
under twenty-five years of age are expected to read for a degree
at one of the many universities old and new; but this is not compulsory and in point of fact fewer and fewer men are doing
so. The Archbishop of York, Dr. Coggan, commenting on a report

* Between 1954 and 1962 a quarter of all the deacons ordained were
over thirty-five years of age.
† Some of these are now to be amalgamated.

194

about the theological colleges, entitled *Theological Colleges For Tomorrow*, which came before the Church Assembly in 1968, said that in the recent past when there were few universities in England more than half the clergy were graduates. Today there were more than twenty-five universities and a greater proportion of the population than ever before was receiving higher education, but among them was growing estrangement from the Christian belief. The proportion of graduates among those ordained had dropped to 35 per cent and seemed likely to drop further.

The Church of England Year Book published at the beginning of 1969 confirmed this statement. Of the 496 ordained deacons in 1967, it declared, only 183 had degrees of any kind, and of that number a mere fifty-seven were graduates of Oxford or Cambridge.

Finally, before a man can be ordained he must procure a title, i.e. the promise of a curacy or some other post in the Church, and be accepted by a bishop. But a deacon still possesses the freedom to choose where he will serve his first curacy, and in exercising this choice he is usually greatly influenced by the principal of his theological college. Attempts however are now being made to institute some sort of direction. It has been suggested, for instance, that each bishop should only ordain the minimum number of men he needs for his own diocese; then 'a candidate who was unable to secure ordination in one particular diocese would be free to apply to any other diocese the quota of which was incomplete'. This arrangement, it was hoped, would lead to a more even distribution of man-power. At the same time a deacon should be strongly encouraged to serve only under an incumbent who could be relied upon to train him thoroughly in his pastoral and priestly duties. The Commission on the Deployment and Payment of the Clergy in their report, *Partners in Ministry*, went a stage further in advocating that the deacon should be deprived of any freedom of choice whatsoever, being 'placed' by a central Church authority, which would be set up to work out a quota system for the diocese as a whole. An up-to-date list of suitable rectors, vicars and their parishes would be kept and men allocated to them for training under the best possible facilities. This thorough training of deacons, the report stresses, must take precedence even over the urgent claims of large industrial areas for man-power. After ordination a deacon would immediately be put on 'the strength' of the diocese, and must serve for at least three years in his first post.

Curates' stipends, following in the wake of inflation, have risen enormously in the last twenty years; and today attempts are being made to pay senior assistants as near as possible the minimum stipend of an incumbent. In 1951 the average deacon received £325 on ordination, and when he was priested £340, which rose by annual increments of £15 to £400, plus a free house for a married man, an allowance of £30 for the first child under six-teen years of age, and usually the Whitsuntide offerings. Ten years later a priest started at £425, rising by £25 increments to a maximum of £500, while the £30 allowances were given for all children of school age. In 1968 the basic wage was £625 in-creasing to £700, which together with child allowances, a free house and Whitsuntide offering gave to the average assistant curate a gross total income of well over a thousand pounds per annum, a fantastic sum when we compare it with that paid to his predecessor only fifty years ago. It continues, of course, to rise with the increased cost of living; but conditions vary enormously from diocese to diocese, and even from parish to parish, which is partly responsible for the drift of curates into the richer but less populated parts of the country. It should be noted in passing that a curate who has been at least fifteen years in holy orders, reached the age of forty and is being paid in accordance with the diocesan scale, is eligible for a supplementary grant from the Church Commissioners of up to £150 a year. These grants are made at the Commissioners' discretion under the Ecclesiastical Commissioners (Provisions for Unbeneficed Clergy) Measures of 1928 and 1931; and require the recommendation of the bishop and the diocesan board of finance. Furthermore all curates who need help, and not simply the older men as of yore, can now obtain a grant of £50 from the Curates' Augmentation Fund, which also provides additional sums for holiday purposes or in an emergency. Between 1931 and 1965 this fund assisted some 5,870 curates.*

Celibacy, which had been the general rule among young curates between the wars, has now gone completely out of fashion and married men predominate. This is partly due to the large increase in older men taking holy orders, but also partly to a general tendency among the young to marry much earlier, which means that ordination candidates are getting married either before or during a stay at a theological college. Out of 576 deacons ordained in 1966, 470 were already married. It therefore behoved incumbents seeking curates to provide them with a free house rather than the old clergyhouse or hospitality at the vicarage; and a curateage has become a permanent feature of most large benefices. This situation also helps to account for the rapid increase in stipends during the post-war period. It was not all loss. A curate's wife could be and normally was an asset to the parish; although an increasingly large number of them go out to work in order to earn the money to buy those many 'extras' that for most people have become necessities. Her position during her husband's training, however, is often far from easy. One such wife wrote in 1969 : 'Instead of being able to enjoy the time at college it is for many ordinands' wives a time of misery and hardship. Sometimes college hours mean that husbands are away from the house from early morning until late at night; in some cases wives have to work in order to keep themselves and their families; and often, because of the hours of their jobs, they hardly see their husbands at all. This coupled with the financial worry can quickly cause a wife to resent her husband's calling and even actively revolt against it. Not a very firm foundation on which a man may build

* The Bishop of Kingston has recently set up the Kingston Trust to assist hard-up assistant curates in the Inner London boroughs.

his ministry. At the end of two or three years' training he can find himself without funds, and with a wife who has lost all her enthusiasm for the work which he is to do.'

After passing their priests' exams, curates are also expected to attend a regular course of study during the first three years of their ministry; and this is likely to be extended and improved upon in the near future. But the swift advance of a curate to an 'independency' of his own, which was a feature of the years immediately following the Second World War, is likely to come to an end as the whole parochial system goes into the melting pot, and its future appears to lie more and more with the large parish groupings rather than the individual benefice. The South Ormsby experiment, consisting of fifteen tiny ecclesiastical bene- fices in the wolds of Lincolnshire, has led the way. Since 1949 these parishes have been grouped together under a single rector, assisted by a couple of married curates, who live in two of the retained vicarages, are priests-in-charge of their own districts, and promise to stay there for at least three years. The success of this venture has led to its being copied in many other parts of the country; and the whole idea has been further developed under the Pastoral Measure 1968 along the lines of what are styled 'team' and 'group' ministeries. The former will include a rector and a number of other ministers with the 'title' of vicar and a status equal to that of an incumbent minus the freehold. The rector would be the leader of the team, which would also employ assistant curates, with a general responsibility for the whole area; and in conjunction with the bishop appoint the vicars, each of whom would be licensed to a particular cure of souls within that district. The latter will comprise a group of incumbents of equal status, who together with their curates would assist one another 'to make the best possible provision for the cure of souls through- out the area of the group ministry'. The future career of the curate, who decides to opt for the parochial system rather than some specialised ministry, probably lies in one or other of these groupings, which are bound sooner or later to absorb most church livings. Here he will be employed as a member of a team rather than attached to any one particular incumbent, gradually working his way up the ladder of promotion until he reaches the dizzy eminence of senior curate or is promoted to one of the titular vicarages. His chances of obtaining the old-time 'independency' is slight, since the single, independent parish, manned by the old-fashioned 'jack-of-all-trades' appears to be on its way out. The number of ordinations, as has already been noted, has steadily declined of recent years; and in its recent report on *The Selection and Training for the Auxiliary Ministry*, A.C.C.M. has suggested a remedy in the ordination of older men, who while pursuing their ordinary secular employments, would serve the Church on a part-time basis, as members of a clerical team. Their ages would range between thirty and fifty, and their selection and training 'should accord with the highest standards possible'. They would not be paid by the Church and could not be eligible for a benefice 'without further scrutiny'. The dangers of such a proposal are obvious : it could lead to the creation of a 'second class' category of clergy, discourage lay-readers, and throw doubt on the value of the full-time ministry, whose standing has already been undermined by the up-grading of the laity, who are now often permitted to perform many priestly functions, such for example as assisting with the communion service. This is but one of many factors that may lead in the future to a drastic reduction in the number of full-time clergy; others include the present theological ferment in the Churches; the growing hostile climate towards religion in society as a whole and the universities in particular; and the increasing 'take-over' of educational, charitable and social work by the State. Furthermore the steady denigration of the status and independence of a still inadequately paid parochial clergy, which the Pastoral Measure of 1968 and the Morley Report, *Partners in Ministry*, have certainly not helped to allay, make the curate's future uncertain. To a self-confident minority of ordination candidates, who demand participation in the running of the theological colleges, this fluid situation may well prove exhilarating, since they feel they can mould it to their own convictions. Such a man, for example, is the Reverend David Hart, an assistant curate of St. Michael's, Highgate, whose organisation, *Church*, occupied St. Mark's, North Audley Street, Mayfair, one Saturday night during 1968 for what was described as a 'requiem for Vietnam'. They did so on the following grounds : 'that this chapel is a symbol of the Established Church's complicity in the Vietnam War and our action today is to oppose that complicity. By complicity we mean the active and passive collaboration between Church and military, the immoral role of religion as a morale-booster and the amoral role of the Church as the universal blind-eye.' Another is the Reverend M. J. Rear, assistant curate of St. Alban's, Hull, who early in 1969 boldly produced an alternative to the official scheme for Anglican-Methodist reunion, which, he claimed, would 'respect the consciences of both Anglo-Catholics and Evangelicals'. But for the 'run-of-the-mill' majority of curates the present position is nothing short of daunting. Allied to these uncertainties is the general anti-institutionalism of much contemporary religious thought; and a growing belief among young men of faith, vision and idealism that perhaps taking orders and becoming part of the Establishment is not now the most fruitful way of serving God and building His Kingdom.

On the obverse side of the medal we find that curates are being looked after by the Church authorities as never before, their interests protected and their financial position secured; while the relationship between an incumbent and his assistants is happier than it has ever been : labouring side by side in the vineyard as brothers and equals, addressing one another by their christian names, equally zealous in their common role as *servi servorum Dei*.

Such is the present picture; but the winds of change are blowing so fiercely through the Establishment that the position may well be out-dated before these pages appear in print.

In its report, *Ordained Ministry Today*, published by the

CONCLUSION (1945-69)

Advisory Council for the Church's Ministry in 1969, the authors
wrote :

The traditional pattern of clerical education equipped men for a
(typically solo) incumbent ministry in a stereotyped parochial structure. We need an orientation from the start towards a *shared* ministry, towards team-work between priests and active laity, team-work
among priests themselves. For this careful training is needed. And
we need an orientation towards adaptability of the ordained role
to a wide variety of situations, not all of them foreseen by any means
when the initial training takes place.

Appendices

APPENDIX TO CHAPTER III

READERS

The shortage of clergy at the beginning of Elizabeth's reign and the lack of suitable candidates coming forward for ordination were partly alleviated by the experiment of appointing lay readers, lectores, to serve in small parishes or assist over-worked incumbents in the larger towns, especially in London. Strype tells us in his *Annals* that 'they were to be taken out of the laity, tradesmen and others; any that was of sober conversation and honest behaviour, and could read or write . . . they seemed not wholly to forbear their callings, but were not countenanced to follow them, especially if they were mechanical'. They were not licensed like a curate, but merely 'tolerated'; and the document that they received when they were commissioned was called a 'toleration'. A sharp eye was kept upon them and every six months they were expected to submit a testimony of their good behaviour 'from the honest in the parish'. Furthermore on his admission a reader was ordered to enter into a bond to pay £20 to one of the bishop's officers if he should violate the terms of his contract. Under this bond he promised as follows : 'that he the above-bounden N.N. being tolerated and admitted to read prayers in the church or chapel of N . . . according to the Book of Common Prayer, together with the chapters and suffrages appointed by the same, do not in anything or things touching his said office contrary or otherwise than in the said book specified and allowed, then the present obligation to be void and of none effect, or else to stand and remain in full force'.

They were allowed to read prayers, bury the dead and church women, but were not permitted to preach and expound the scriptures or to administer the sacraments. Inevitably some of them overstepped their privileges : Stephen Bouth, reader of Revesby, was presented in 1585 because 'he baptizes and celebrates matrimony'; while in the Lincoln Liber Cleri of 1603, 1604 and 1607 a number of readers are actually classified as either 'incumbent' or 'curate'. In the larger towns their ability to take funerals must have been of considerable help to incumbents at a time when the mortality rate was so high.

However, the experiment as a whole was not a successful one and was gradually discontinued as the supply of clergy increased. There were, for example, some thirty-eight readers in the Lincoln diocese in 1585, but this number had been reduced to fourteen by 1614, ten of whom were ultimately ordained. This last was unusual since most readers did not reach the educational standard required by the bishops for ordination. They simply disappeared back into the ranks of the laity.

APPENDIX TO CHAPTER V

The following account of the case of the chapel in the hamlet of Hadnall's Ease, which was part of the parish of Myddle, Shropshire, recorded by Richard Gough in his *Antiquities and Memoirs* about the year 1700, is a good example of the difficulties experienced by the congregation of such a chapel of ease in securing from the incumbent of the mother church an adequate stipend for the curate-in-charge :

HADNALL CHAPPEL

This chapel was built by the ancestors of the inhabitants of Hadnall's Ease, and is a chappel of ease as appears. First because no other persons have any seats or kneeling within this chappel, save only the inhabitants of Hadnall's Ease. Secondly, because there is no allowance or maintenance for a minister there, save only what is given as a free gift. Thirdly, because the inhabitants of Hadnell's Ease do maintain and repair this chappel at their own proper charges, and yet they doe pay Leawans to the churchwardens of Myddle for the repairing of the parish church. The inhabitants of Hadnall's Ease have endeavoured several times to get an allowance from the rector of Myddle for the maintenance of their minister, and also to have seats in Myddle church, but their endeavours have proved ineffectual. The last time they endeavoured was by a petition, presented to the Reverend Bishop, Dr. Lloyde, formerly Bishop of St. Asaph, and then Bishop of Coventry and Lichfield, and now Bishop of Worcester. . . . The petition concerning Hadnall's Ease was presented to the said Bishop by some of the inhabitants of Hadnall at Shrewsbury, in his primary visitation of this part of his Diocese of Coventry and Lichfield.

APPENDICES

HADNALL PETITION

The Humble Petition of the inhabitants of the Chappelldry of Hadnall, in the Parish of Myddle, in the county of Salop, within your Lordship's Diocese, humbly sheweth, that whereas your Petitioners, being thirty families, and three long myles distant from the Mother church of Myddle, and having a chappell at Hadnall, which your petitioners doe maintaine at your petitioners own charge, and likewise doe contribute a fourth part towards the maintenance of the said Church of Myddle, and whereas the tythes of your said petitioners' estates, within the said Chappelldry being a fourth part of the said parish are worth fifty pounds per annum; and your petitioners having noe seates in the said parish Church of Myddle, to have divine service, and to participate of the holy sacraments.

Your parishioners doe humbly pray that your Lordship, out of your religious care for the welfare of your petitioners in the premisses would be pleased to order the present incumbent to provide for your petitioners a competent curate to read divine service, and administer the holy sacrament to your petitioners, or to make such reasonable allowance, for the maintenance of such a Curate, as your Lordship, in your most pyouse charity, shall think fitt.

MY LORD BISHOP'S ANSWEARE, *Adbaston, 21st Aug. 1693*

Gentlemen, Having spoken with Mr. Dale concerning your demand, and a better allowance for the Chappell of Hadnall, hee told mee hee is not bound to make any allowance, because it is only a chappell of ease built by your ancestors for their own better convenience; and that there was never anything paid towards the serving of that chappell by any of his predecessors. However, hee did of his own accord give five pounds a year, and so much hee is willing to continue as long as you will take it of free gift, but if you will stand with him for more, you shall have only what the law will give you.

This being the sume of his answeare, as I understand it, I thought good to acquaint you with this to the end that if you can prove any contract for the payment of any salary to your curate by the Rector of Myddle, or if you can prove such custom of payment, you will acquaint me with it, for by either of these you may oblige the present Rector to do what has been done formerly; but, if that which you desire bee a new thing without either contract or custom, it is not in my power to impose it; and at present, this being a time of extraordinary payments, I know not how to persuade him to it. . . .

I am your assured friend and servant,

W. Cov. & Lich.

To my respected friends, the Inhabitants of the Chappelry of Hadnall, in the parish of Myddle.

205

APPENDICES

This paper contains a true copy of a petition delivered to my Lord Bishop of Coventry and Lichfield by the inhabitants of Hadnall, in his Lordship's primary visitation, held in the yeare 1693, together with his Lordship's answeare thereunto, being both compared and examined by us.
5th Sept. 1699.

Fra. Evans. Not. Pub.
Thomas Hughes. Not. Public.

Select Bibliography

CHAPTERS I AND II

Bowker, Margaret, *The Secular Clergy in the Diocese of Lincoln, 1495–1520*, 1968.

Chadwick, D., *Social Life in the Days of Piers Plowman*, 1922. *Chaucer's Canterbury Tales for the Modern Reader*, ed. Arthur Burrell, 1930.

Coulton, G. G., *Parish Life in Medieval England*, 1907. *The Medieval Village*, 1925. *Medieval Panorama*, 1938.

Cutts, E. L., *Parish Priests and their People*, 1898.

Deanesley, Margaret, *Pre-Conquest Church in England*, 1961.

Gasquet, F. A., *Parish Life in Medieval England*, 1906.

Godfrey, John, *The English Parish, 600–1300*, 1969.

Haines, R. M., *The Administration of the Diocese of Worcester in the first half of the Fourteenth Century*, 1965.

Hartridge, R. A. R., *A History of Vicarages in the Middle Ages*, 1930.

Heath, P., *English Parish Clergy on the Eve of the Reformation*, 1969.

Moorman, J. R. H., *Church Life in England in the Thirteenth Century*, 1945.

Pantin, W. A., *The English Church in the Fourteenth Century*, 1955.

Powys, A. R., *The English Parish Church*, 1930.

Richardson, H. G., *The Parish Clergy of the Thirteenth and Fourteenth Centuries* (*Transactions of the Royal Historical Society*, Vol. VI. 1912).

Smith, A. Maynard, *Pre-Reformation England*, 1963.

The Book Concerning Piers Plowman, ed. R. Attwater, 1957.

Thompson, A. Hamilton, *The English Clergy*, 1947.

Visitations in the Diocese of Lincoln, 1517–1531 (Lincoln Record Society), ed A. Hamilton Thompson, 1940.

SELECT BIBLIOGRAPHY

Wilkins, D., *Concilia*, 1737.

Wood-Legh, K. L., *Studies in English Church Life under Edward III*, 1934. *Perpetual Chantries in Britain*, 1965.

CHAPTER III

Barratt, D. M., *The condition of the Parochial Clergy between the Reformation and 1660* (unpublished Ph. D. thesis, Oxford).

Bishop Redman's Visitation, 1597 (Norfolk Record Society), ed. J. F. Williams, 1946.

Brooks, F. W., *The Social Position of the Parson in the Sixteenth Century* (Journal of the Archaeological Association, 3rd Series, X, 1945–7).

Cardwell, E., *Documentary Annals*, 2 vols, 1853.

Correspondence of Archbishop Parker (Parker Society), 1853.

Depositions and other Ecclesiastical Proceedings from the Courts of Durham (Surtees Society), 1845.

Dickens, A. G., *The English Reformation*, 1964.

Ecclesiastical Proceedings of Bishop Barnes (Surtees Society), ed. J. Raines, 1850.

Edwards, A. C., *English History from Essex Sources*, 2 vols (Essex Record Society), 1952.

Essex Parish Records, 1240–1894 (Essex Record Society), ed. E. J. Erith, 1950.

Frere, W. H., *The Marian Reaction in its Relation to the English Clergy*, 1896. *The English Church in the Reigns of Elizabeth and James I*, 1904.

Gee, H., *The Elizabethan Clergy*, 1898.

Hoskyns, W. G., *The Leicestershire Country Parson in the Sixteenth Century* (The Leicestershire Archaeological Society), 1940.

Kennedy, W. M., *Elizabethan Episcopal Administration*, 3 vols (Alcuin Society), 1924.

Knappen, M. M., *Tudor Puritanism*, 1939. *Two Elizabethan Puritan Diaries*, 1930.

Lincoln Episcopal Records in the Time of Thomas Cooper (Lincoln Record Society), 1912.

Neale, Daniel, *The History of the Puritans*, 5 vols, 1822.

Peters, Robert, *Oculi Episcopi: Administration in the Archdeaconry of St Albans, 1580–1625,* 1963.

Remains of Archbishop Grindal (Parker Society), 1843.

Sermons of Bishop Latimer, 2 vols (Parker Society), 1844–5.

SELECT BIBLIOGRAPHY

Strype, J., *Annals of The Reformation*, 4 vols, 1824.

Tate, W. E., *The Parish Chest*, 1948.

The Archdeacon's Court, 1584, 2 vols (Oxfordshire Record Society), ed. E. R. C. Brinkworth, 1942–6.

The State of the Church in the Reigns of Elizabeth and James I (Lincoln Record Society), ed. C. W. Foster, 1926.

Tudor Parish Documents of the Diocese of York, ed. J. S. Purvis, 1948.

Tyler, Philip, *The Status of the Elizabethan Parochial Clergy* (Studies in Church History vol. IV), ed. G. J. Cuming, 1947.

Wilson, H. A., *Constitutions and Canons Ecclesiastical, 1604*, 1923.

Winchester Consistory Court Depositions (Hampshire Record Society), ed. A. J. Willis, 1960.

Works of Archbishop Whitgift, vol. I (Parker Society), 1851.

CHAPTER IV

Addy, J., *The Archdeacon and Ecclesiastical Discipline in Yorkshire, 1598–1714: Clergy and Churchwardens*, 1963.

A Hampshire Miscellany. I: Metropolitical Visitation of Winchester, 1607–1608, ed. J. A. Willis, 1963.

Ashley, M., *Life in Stuart England*, 1964.

Autobiography of Richard Baxter, ed. T. J. M. Lloyd, 1925.

A Viewe of the State of the Clargie within the Countie of Essex, 1604.

Calendar of the Committee of Compounding, 1643–1660, 2 vols., 1889–90.

Collectanea II (Somerset Record Society), ed. T. F. Palmer, 1928.

Diary of the Revd. Ralph Josselin (Camden Society), ed. E. Hockliffe, 1908.

Episcopal Visitation Book for the Archdeaconry of Buckingham (Buckingham Record Society), ed. E. R. C. Brinkworth, 1947.

Gough, R., *Human Nature Displayed in the History of Myddle*, ed W. G. Hoskins, 1968.

Hart, A. Tindal, *William Lloyd*, 1952.

Hill, C., *Economic Problems of the Church From Archbishop Whitgift to the Long Parliament*, 1956. *The Century of Revolution*, 1961. *Society and Puritanism in Pre-Reformation England*, 1964.

Hood, C. D., *Sequestered Loyalists and Bartholomew Sufferers*, 1922.

Jukes, H. A. Lloyd, *Matthew Wren* (an unpublished thesis).

o

SELECT BIBLIOGRAPHY

Marchant, R., *The Puritans and the Church Courts in the Diocese of York, 1560–1642*, 1960.

Matthews, A. G., *Calamy Revised*, 1934. *Walker Revised*, 1948.

Oxfordshire Peculiars (Oxfordshire Record Society), ed. S. A. Peyton, 1928.

Pemberton, W. A., *Studies in the Ecclesiastical Court and Archdeaconry of Nottingham, 1660–1689* (unpublished Ph. D. thesis, Nottingham University).

Proceedings Principally in the County of Kent (Camden Society), ed. L. B. Larking, 1862.

Sykes, N., *From Sheldon to Secker*, 1959.

The Autobiography of Henry Newcombe, 2 vols. (Chetham Society), ed. R. Parkinson, 1852.

The Churchwardens Presentments in the Seventeenth Century. Parts I & II: Archdeaconry of Chichester and Archdeaconry of Lewes (Sussex Record Society), ed. Hilda Johnstone, 1947–8, 1948–9.

The Committee at Stafford, 1643–1645 (Stafford Record Society), ed. D. H. Pennington and I. A. Roots, 1958.

The County Committee of Kent in the Civil War, ed. A. M. Everitt, 1958.

The Curates' Conference (*The Harleian Miscellany*. vol. IV., 1808).

The Life of Adam Martindale (Chetham Society), ed. R. Parkinson, 1845.

Trotter, E., *Seventeenth Century Life in the Country Parish*, 1919.

CHAPTER V

Archbishop Herring's Visitation Returns, 1743, ed. S. L. Ollard and P. C. Walker, 5 vols., 1928.

Articles of Enquiry Addressed to the Clergy of the Diocese of Oxford at the Primary Visitation of Dr. Thomas Secker, 1738, ed. H. A. Lloyd Jukes, 1957.

Best, G. F. A., *Temporal Pillars*, 1964.

Church and Countryside, 1953.

Diary of a Country Parson: The Reverend James Woodforde, ed. J. Beresford. Vol. I. 1758–81, 1924.

Diary of the Revd. William Jones, ed. O. F. Christie, 1929.

Derry, Warren, *Dr. Parr*, 1966.

Hart, A. Tindal, *The Life and Times of John Sharp, Archbishop of York*, 1949. *The Country Parson in the Eighteenth Century*, 1955. *Country Counting House*, 1962.

SELECT BIBLIOGRAPHY

Journal of the Rev. William Bagshaw Stevens, ed. Georgina Galbraith, 1965.

Legg, J. Wickham, *English Church Life from the Restoration to the Tractarian Movement*, 1914.

Savidge, Alan, *The Foundation and Early Years of Queen Anne's Bounty*, 1955.

Speculum Dioeceseos Lincolniensis sub Episcopis Gul: Wake et Edm: Gibson, Part I. 1705–23, ed. R. E. G. Cole, 1913.

Stackhouse, T., *The Miseries and Great Hardships of the Inferior Clergy in and about London*, 1722.

Sykes, N., *Church and State in the Eighteenth Century*, 1934.

The Gentleman's Magazine, 1731 onwards.

The Parson in English Literature, ed. F. E. Christmas, 1950.

Tyerman, G. M., *Life and Times of the Revd. Samuel Wesley*, 1866.

Warne, A., *Church and Society in Eighteenth-Century Devon*, 1969.

CHAPTER VI

A Norfolk Diary, ed. H. P. J. Armstrong, 1949.

Baring-Gould, S., *Old Country Life*, 1890. *Early Reminiscences*, 1923.

Battiscombe, Georgina, *John Keble*, 1963.

Bishop Wilberforce's Visitation Returns for the Archdeaconry of Oxford, (Oxfordshire Record Society) ed. E. P. Baker, 1954.

Bloom, Ursula, *Parson Extraordinary*, 1963.

Brown, C. K. F., *A History of the English Clergy*, 1954.

Bullock, F. W. B., *A History of the Training for the Ministry of the Church of England, 1800–1874*, 1955.

Chadwick, Owen, *Victorian Miniature*, 1960. *The Victorian Church*, Part I, 1966.

Church Congress Reports 1867.

Clive, Mary, *Caroline Clive*, 1949.

Coombs, Joyce, *William Henry Whitworth, 1834–85* (*The Church Quarterly Review*, April-June 1967).

Cripps, H. W., *A Practical Treatise on the law relating to the Church and Clergy*, 8th edition, 1937.

Eliot, George, *Scenes from Clerical Life*.

Ellman, E. B., *Recollections of a Sussex Parson*, 1925.

SELECT BIBLIOGRAPHY

Inglis, K. S., *Churches and the Working Classes in Victorian England*, 1963.

Jordan, J., *A Curate's Views of Church Reform (Thoughts on the Sabbath)*, ed. R. Whately, 1837.

Mayor, Stephen, *The Churches and the Labour Movement*, 1967.

McClatchey, Diana, *Oxfordshire Clergy, 1777–1869*, 1960.

My Curates by a Rector, 1890.

My Rectors by a Quondam Curate, 1890.

Pickard-Cambridge, A. W., *Memoir of the Reverend Octavius Pickard-Cambridge*, 1918.

Plomer, William, *Diary of the Revd. Francis Kilvert*, 3 vols., 1969.

Scott, D. L., *A Century Ago in a Country Parish (The Modern Churchman*, June, 1951).

The Whole Case of the Unbeneficed Clergy: by a Presbyter of the Church, 2nd edition, 1843.

Trollope, Anthony, *Clergymen of the Church of England*, 1866.

Stephenson, A. G. M., *The First Lambeth Conference*, 1967.

Unpublished Diary of the Revd. Richard Seymour, Curacies 1832–35.

Unpublished Diary of the Revd. Robert Hart, Curacies 1860–69.

Webster, A. B., *Joshua Watson*, 1954.

Wickham, E. R., *Church and People in an Industrial City*, 1969 edition.

Wingfield-Stratford, E., *This Was a Man*, 1949.

Young, M. B., *Richard Wilton, a forgotten Victorian*, 1967.

CHAPTERS VII AND VIII

Carpenter, E. F., *The Service of a Parson*, 1965.

Chichester Diocesan Calendar and Directory, 1900–1969.

Church Congress Reports.

Crockford Prefaces, 1947 onwards.

Curates Augmentation Fund Minute Books, 1866–1969.

Ferris, Paul, *The Church of England*, 1964.

Gummer, Selwyn, *The Chavasse Twins*, 1963.

Lloyd, Roger, *The Church of England, 1900–1965*, 1966.

Lockhart, J. G., *Cosmo Gordon Lang*, 1949.

Ordained Ministry Today, 1969.

Partners in Ministry, 1967.

Pastoral Measure, 1967.

Paul, Leslie, *The Deployment and Payment of the Clergy*, 1964.

SELECT BIBLIOGRAPHY

Sheen, H. E., *Canon Peter Green*, 1965.

Smith, A. C., *The South Ormsby Experiment*, 1960.

Smyth, Charles, *Cyril Foster Garbett*, 1959.

The Church of England Year Book, 1900–1969.

The Church Times.

The English Church: A New Look, ed. L. S. Hunter, 1966.

Theological Colleges for Tomorrow, 1968.

West, Frank, *The Country Parish Today and Tomorrow*, 1960.

Index

215

INDEX

INDEX

INDEX

INDEX

INDEX